RUN *PATTY* RUN

Tantrums, Toads, and Teddy Bears

RUN *PATTY* RUN

The Story of a Very Special Long-Distance Runner
Who Lights the Way for Others

SHEILA CRAGG

with **Jim, Dotty and Patty Wilson**

HARPER & ROW, PUBLISHERS

SAN FRANCISCO

Cambridge
Hagerstown
Philadelphia
New York

1817

London
Mexico City
São Paulo
Sydney

FIRST EDITION

Designed by Jim Mennick

Library of Congress Cataloging in Publication Data
Cragg, Sheila.
   RUN PATTY RUN.
   1. Wilson, Patty.   2. Runners (Sports)—United States—Biography.   3. Epileptics—Biography.
I. Title.
GV697.W5G7   796.4'26 [B]   78-20583
ISBN 0–06–250160–7

---

80 81 82 83 84 10 9 8 7 6 5 4 3 2 1

To two of my friends,

Roy M. Carlisle and *Karen Ann Wojahn,*

who sharpened my skills and so generously contributed
their great gifts to me and to this book

Special Dedication

To my father, who started my running, and my family, who kept me going.

—PATTY WILSON

We would especially like to thank the organizations, businesses, and people listed below, who have generously supported us throughout the years chronicled by this book. There is, of course, no way to list all the thousands of wonderful people who have helped us on our journey, but to all of them we say a special thank you.

—THE WILSON FAMILY

John Baker
Bob Bradach
John Loftus

Epilepsy Center of Oregon
Epilepsy Foundation of America
Kaiser Permanente Hospital
National Football League Players
  Association
Preventive and Sports Medicine
  Center

Allstate Insurance Company

Allstate Life Company
Blue Ribbon Sports–Nike
Coachman Industries
Dale's R.V. Rentals
Jelenk
Master Runner
Muller Chemical, Inc.
Nutriscience, Inc.
Porvene, Inc.
Real Estate Shoppe

Contents

Preface

A "CHANCE" meeting altered the course of my writing career.
While browsing in a yardage store, I met the director of the Orange
County Epilepsy Society over a bolt of material. She mentioned that
a young girl and her father were running one thousand miles from
Southern California to Portland, Oregon. The purpose of her extraordinary goal was two-fold: she was eager to break her own
long-distance record; and because she had epilepsy, she wanted her
running to "stand for something." She hoped to help people understand what epilepsy was all about.

After meeting Patty Wilson and her family, I recognized the opportunity to do something I had been attempting for several years:
to break the print barrier that seemed to surround the word "epilepsy."

Patty impressed me with her genuine interest in epilepsy and its
consequences, not merely because she has this disorder, but because
she cares about people and their rights. Beyond that, I admired her
courage and her willingness to make herself vulnerable to the public
when to do so went against her private nature. Like others who have
championed the rights of the minority despite personal risk or conse-
quence, Patty has chosen to be a symbol for people who have epilepsy.

Why was it so important for me to write Patty's story and to have
a part in changing the myths and prejudices that still haunt this closet
disorder? Our son has epilepsy.

I was concerned that Patty and he and the two million or more
people who share their problem have the right to live their lives like

other people, without the special laws and regulations which currently hinder their freedom. I wanted to voice their right to secure employment without deception, to obtain drivers' licences and life, health, and automobile insurance at reasonable rates, and to participate in American society without arbitrary limitations.

Patty and I never imagined the far-reaching results of her story. *Reader's Digest* condensed "Patty Wilson's Magnificent Marathon," an article originally published in *Family Weekly,* and sent it around the world in its international editions. *Lady's Circle* and three textbook companies also reprinted her story.

Subsequently, in 1978, Herald Press published *Tantrums, Toads, and Teddy Bears,* a book about our son's struggle to win over nonconvulsive epilepsy and hyperactivity.

Through *run Patty run* we hope the word epilepsy will be "spoken with dignity and echoed courageously." We are lighting the Candle of Understanding, and it is flickering brightly.

Acknowledgments

No WRITER gives birth to a book alone. Without the skills and perspectives of the following people, this project would surely have been stillborn. Clayton Carlson, publisher, and Marie Cantlon, editorial director, were committed to the story from the beginning. Kathy Reigstad, production editor, translated that commitment into constant encouragement.

My husband Ron and our two sons undergirded me with their love, while Karen Ann Wojahn, Leona Ross, Dorothea Marvin Nyberg, and Carole Gift Page sustained me with editorial guidance and warm friendship. Scott DeGarmo, former editor of *Family Weekly,* started it all when he published "Patty Wilson's Magnificent Marathon."

Yet it was Roy M. Carlisle, my editor, who stretched my thinking and taught me. He gave generous and faithful support to me and to this project.

This is my offering of thanks to those who, because they believed in me, have helped this book come to life.

The silver shoes . . . have wonderful powers. And one of the most curious things about them is that they can carry you to any place in the world in three steps, and each step will be made in the wink of an eye. All you have to do is to knock the heels together three times and command the shoes to carry you wherever you wish to go.

L. Frank Baum
The Wizard of Oz

1 *Odd One Out*

THE two-mile course was no simple maze a mouse could run through. Because it was a confusing network of crisscrossing paths, Patty walked the chalk-marked course before the race. If she were to trail behind as she usually did, she could lose her way.

It was the first preseason cross-country event, and four high schools were competing at a park in La Mirada, California. Patty was the only girl among fifty runners, and at thirteen, she was one of the youngest. The boys were milling around; some were shaking their arms and legs to loosen up; others were doing wind sprints.

While Patty did her stretching exercises, she had difficulty breathing. The air she inhaled was a sweltering, smoggy, ninety degrees. The afternoon sun was red, and the thick and acrid salmon-colored air irritated her eyes.

When Patty heard the starter shout, "Last call!" she felt a twinge of nervousness. Suddenly she couldn't remember which way they were going to run, so she squeezed through the tangle of boys jockeying for position. She wanted to be near the front, so as not to fall behind.

At the starting line, Patty wiped the dampness from her face, then tightened the band restraining her waist-length hair. She knelt to tie her shoes again, making sure they were triple knotted. Then she pulled up her knee socks and straightened her shorts. Waiting tensely, she shifted from foot to foot, intently watching the starter.

When the gunshot cracked the air, Patty dashed out with the front group of runners. The last thing she recalled was her father reminding her not to start off too fast; after that she didn't remember anything.

Following along the sidelines, Jim and Dotty Wilson wondered why their daughter was running so strangely. A quarter mile out, Patty started running mechanically; her arms and legs swung stiffly. She didn't seem to be breathing; her chest was still, giving no sign that she was inhaling or exhaling. Her head was motionless—no strained facial movements, no squinting, nothing! She seemed to be running on an inner, automatic control. Jim and Dotty were stunned by the sudden realization that Patty was having a seizure.

They panicked. They couldn't tell the officials to halt the race. To pull Patty out of the pack of runners would have been like running into the Indianapolis 500 to stop one car. Jim fled along the perimeter of the course to watch her, to rescue her if she fell. He was astounded; she was running the tortuous course as if she'd photographed it.

Then, about three hundred feet from the finish, Patty started cutting across the course, veering toward another path. A thicket of runners was still between Patty and Jim. Even if he could get near her, he couldn't touch her or he'd disqualify her. He galloped down the sidelines, waving and flapping his hands.

"Back on the road! Patty! Back on the road!" he yelled.

Her brother, Richard, on the opposite side, saw Patty moving in the wrong direction. He chased her, pointing and shouting.

"That way! Go that way, Patty!"

Richard's frantic gestures somehow relayed their intention to her internal control system, and she turned and dashed toward the finish. She was on automatic pilot again, sprinting faster than she ever had. Perhaps the movement of the runners, the voices of her father and brother, and the cheering crowd stimulated her semiconscious body to speed up.

She still wasn't breathing heavily. Her lips were only slightly open, her eyes still vacant. Her face lacked animation. Despite her marching, mechanical style, she sped past boys who were stretching up and out for the final burst across the line. Their jaws slack, sweat streamed down their flushed faces and bodies.

Patty darted across the finish line in ninth place. Her coach, her teammates, and her family congratulated her.

"You were really smoking!" the guys exclaimed.

They didn't know Patty had had a partial complex seizure, and she didn't know why they were thumping her and shaking her hand. She appeared to respond to their congratulations. She seemed to be conscious, but she wasn't; she was completely unaware of what was happening. Like a dazed boxer, she was knocked out, but still standing.

She didn't know why people were talking to her, where she was, or that she'd run a race. Jim and Dotty didn't understand how Patty had been able to run faster during a seizure, or why she could continue without falling.

Although it was on her school records, Jim and Dotty hadn't told anyone that Patty had epilepsy. Jim had to fight to get her on the boys' cross-country team because she was a girl; now he feared they'd kick her off the team if they found out about her seizure and her epilepsy.

Jim and Dotty quietly steered her away from the crowd and took her to a drinking fountain. They cooled her off and walked her around. Patty didn't know what color the grass was, or what her mother's name was. Was the sky up in the air and the ground below? She didn't know!

"What's your name?" Jim asked. "Do you know who I am? Where do you live? Are you a girl?"

Patty didn't respond. She didn't know the answer to any of Jim's simple questions. She realized he was talking to her, but she couldn't hear his voice, and she couldn't speak.

Dotty and Jim knew she was returning to consciousness when she responded to a game he played with her. He held a finger up to see if she could match him with the same finger. Then he'd hold up a second finger and a third. When she was finally able to match his finger, they were relieved. It was forty minutes before she came out of it.

Every time Patty had a seizure, a portion of her life was lost, missing forever. Like an orphan who can only ask about but never know his parents, Patty would have to relive this race through the memory of others. It was disappointing to her; she was robbed of a treasured victory. The thief, epilepsy, would never return it to her.

Patty's doctor said she could continue running if she had someone with her. Jim had always run every mile she ran, and she was happiest running with him. He was more than her father; he was the friend she yearned for, the one person she could really talk to. For Jim, selling insurance was something he had to do to pay bills. But he preferred running with Patty or watching any one of his children competing in a sport. Since Richard ran cross-country, too, he'd be with Patty whenever their parents were unable to be there. They determined to let her continue running.

Jim wondered why he encouraged Patty to run. He worried that she would seriously injure herself. It scared him when she had a seizure running; so strong was his fear that he could scarcely bring himself to think about it. Jim reminded himself why he'd first encouraged her to compete in cross-country and track events.

He slipped back three years to when Patty was in sixth grade, to the first time he'd really believed she could run. The memory of the day he'd set his challenge at her feet was vivid; he could still see her sitting on the porch, dangling her tennis shoes by the strings.

"How come you don't have your shoes on? I thought you were running today," he asked her.

"I don't feel like it, Daddy."

Jim surveyed her face. He knew the look; he knew she'd been excluded again. That angered him. "Put your shoes on, Patty. We can talk while we're running." Her light green shirt and shorts highlighted her hazel eyes. Her long tawny hair fell like a mane over her forehead and shoulders; she brushed it from her face, then tied it into a ponytail.

When she stood up, she looked tiny next to her father's six-foot frame. Muscled, disciplined, and trained, he seemed to her to be the super athlete. In fact, her whole family were super athletes, as two walls of trophies testified. Everyone but her.

Patty and he ran silently, crossing neighboring streets. Jim ran smoothly. His massive arms and legs pumped like well-oiled pistons. Perspiration flattened his thick, almost black hair. Jim noticed the easily missed sign that announced *La Palma,* marking their otherwise invisible Southern California city boundary. Their neighborhood, with its one- and two-story stuccoed homes and well manicured lawns, was framed by circular streets. Wood skeletons of half-built housing tracts stood too close to each other. Old and new homes, Mexican barrios, small clusters of orange trees and empty barns—these the last remnants of dairies and ranches—sprawled here and there among the new tracts.

Ordinarily when Jim and Patty ran together, she chattered about her day. Today she was silent, sober, downcast. She was thinking about what had just happened. She'd been watching the neighborhood boys and her sister play ball. Patty thought about the way her sister, Sandy—everyone called her Sam—deftly scooped up the ball and tagged Richard out.

I don't care. So what if they won't let me play ball. she told herself.

Then she remembered what had happened with Carol Anderson and Jenny Baker* an hour earlier. They had refused to play with her. Patty sighed. She wished she could be Jenny, who was so slim and pretty and popular. Patty and Jenny had been friends since second grade, but now Jenny only played with Carol. Patty hated being left out. Loneliness welled up in her, and it felt terrible. She wanted to cry, but she held back her tears.

Jim glanced at Patty. He didn't like seeing her this way, especially during their special time together. They usually laughed and joked and called each other silly names.

"What's going on?" he asked, hoping she would tell him. Maybe she'd feel better.

"The guys won't let me play ball. They laugh at me and tell me, 'You throw like a klutz.' I try to throw like the guys, like Sam, but I can't."

Jim pictured the rag doll way Patty threw the ball off target. He could see her in her catcher's vest, face mask, and mitt playing girl's softball. She was afraid of the ball; she dodged it and missed it most of the time. How could he console her, help her? He couldn't stand to see her fail like this. He wanted her to feel equal to the other kids.

---

*Names have been changed.

"When I went to Jenny's house today," Patty paused, trying to close out the pain, "I asked if she could play, but they said, 'She's not home.' A few minutes later I saw her leave. Jenny used to be my best friend. Now she doesn't like me."

Even now, while they ran, Jim watched the gawky way her legs flailed. She bounced and jagged like a partially-deflated basketball.

"Dad-dy!"

"I'm sorry, Patty. I was listening to you."

"Tell me about the fifties, when you were in high school," Patty giggled, changing the subject. "Did you have fun?"

My optimistic Patty, Jim thought. *She always bounces back.*

"Those days weren't very happy for me," he replied. "I was lonely. My mother worked in a defense plant and Nana worked at a department store, so I was left alone. My dad had died, so I didn't have a father. I was self-conscious. I hated myself because I was ugly, so I'd do anything in the world to avoid having my picture taken."

"You're not ugly, Daddy."

"I thought I was. I used to listen to my favorite radio program, *Jack Armstrong, the All American Boy.* He was my idol."

Jim stopped suddenly in the middle of the sidewalk, closed his fist, and put it up to his mouth like a microphone. "The announcer used to say, 'Train to be an American! Follow Jack Armstrong's rules for physical fitness: First, get plenty of fresh air, sleep, and exercise; second, use lots of soap and water every day; and third, eat the kind of breakfast America needs in times like these—milk, fruit, and Wheaties—Breakfast of Champions!' "*

"Oh, Daddy," Patty snickered, "that's funny."

"It wasn't to me. I wanted to be physically fit so I could be a champion like Jack Armstrong. That's why I played handball, football, tennis—any sport I could."

"I can't even hit the ball."

"You can run, Patty. Remember Pete Strudwick? The first time I saw him running, do you know what I did?"

"What?"

*Jim Harmon, *The Great Radio Heros* (New York: Doubleday, 1967), p. 245.

"I was driving along and I couldn't believe what I saw, so I put the car in reverse and backed up an entire block. Here was this man with no feet, running down the street. I didn't know it then, but he had foam pads with socks pulled over them and bands to hold everything together. I decided right then if he could run with no feet, I could run."

"One time when you took Mom and Richard and Sam and me down to the high school to run," said Patty, "Pete was running around the track. I asked him, 'How many laps have you run?' He said, 'Thirteen.' I thought, Wow! That seemed forever, I could only do one lap half running and half walking."

"You can run now. We've put in two miles already."

"We haven't!" Patty stopped mid-stride and looked around. "Where are we?"

"See?" Jim's eyes glistened. "Patty, I want you to start training with me. We'll run farther than anyone else has ever run. Maybe we'll run across the United States." He smiled. "Just stick with me, Patty. One day I'll make you a star."

2 *The Word Is Finally Spoken*

DURING the following weeks, Jim agonized each time Patty and he ran together. Her awkwardness was painful to him. *Have I made a mistake, promised her too much?* To remind himself why she had to succeed—to feel success, to know it, to live with it—he played her life through his memory like a movie. It always returned to the same scene, the October Patty was eleven months old.

That autumn had been a typical Southern California Indian summer, with long lighted days and open-windowed evenings. One night it was after ten o'clock before a breath off the ocean cooled and freshened the stale hot air.

"When are you going to sleep, little girl?" Dotty spoke wearily and watched Patty rock back and forth, holding onto her crib rail. "I wonder if she's cutting teeth?" Dotty half-questioned Jim.

Patty reached out and clamped onto her father's shirt.

"You think I'm going to pick you up." Jim smiled and swung Patty up into his arms. Patty squirmed and wiggled to be put down.

"You're as busy as your Daddy," Dotty laughed.

"Let her play. She'll sleep when she's tired." Jim put Patty on the floor and she scooted away.

"Maybe she'll be ready to settle down after I clean up," replied Dotty.

"Patty and I'll watch the late sports news," Jim teased, briefly putting his arms around his wife.

Dotty brushed her naturally curly dark-brown hair, washed her face, and removed a remnant of lipstick. Her ivory complexion needed little makeup. Dotty was medium-boned, with a softly curving silhouette, a stark contrast to Jim's chiseled features and athletic frame. Their only similarity was the hazel eyes they shared with Patty.

Patty crawled into the bathroom and patted her mother's leg. Dotty picked her up and cuddled her. "Your brother's been asleep for hours," Dotty whispered. "You can hardly keep your eyes open." Dotty laid Patty on the double bed. "Patty what are you staring—?"

Patty's eyes rolled back and her eyelids fluttered.

"Jim! *Jim!* Something's wrong with Patty!"

Jim and Dotty stood stunned, poised like wax figures, watching their daughter's arms and legs jerk and flail. Perspiration soaked Patty's duckling-feather hair and reddened face. Her entire body convulsed uncontrollably. The sound of a car pulling into the drive next door broke through their shock.

"Jim, see if that's Betty."

Dotty dropped to her knees and laid her arm next to Patty to keep her from falling off the bed. It had only been minutes, but it seemed like hours had passed. Jim and Betty rushed in and bent down beside Dotty.

"She feels warm." Betty stroked Patty's forehead. "She's had a convulsion. Has she been sick?"

"No, not really," Dotty replied. "She was restless tonight and wouldn't sleep."

Patty's body fell limp. She wrinkled her face and squalled. Carefully, Dotty picked up Patty and cradled her in her arms.

"We'd better get her to the hospital," Jim urged.

"The convulsion's over," Betty consoled. "Patty will be all right now. She's probably so exhausted she'll sleep. Babies sometimes have convulsions when they're sick."

Dotty patted the perspiration off Patty and she felt her skin; it was cool, clammy. There was no sign of a fever. By the time Dotty changed Patty's soaked clothing, the child was sound asleep.

"I'll see myself out. Patty will be fine," Betty said reassuringly.

"Thanks! You always seem to know what to do in a crisis." Dotty replied.

Dotty put Patty's bed next to theirs. Throughout the night she lay and listened to Patty's unusually heavy breathing. She was in a deep, almost unwakeable sleep. Dotty welcomed morning when she could take Patty to the doctor, but dreaded finding out that Patty might have a serious problem.

Their doctor confirmed Patty had had a convulsion. "Patty's fever rose so quickly her brain couldn't handle it," he explained. "Just watch her for any signs of fever. It's nothing to be worried about."

Dotty, adaptive and sensible by nature, relaxed and accepted the doctor's assurance that fever-induced convulsions were normal for some children. But Patty's convulsion was indelibly imprinted on Dotty's memory and every time three-year-old Richard or Patty showed any signs of illness, Dotty checked Patty's temperature for fear she'd have another convulsion.

The memory had almost vanished by the time Sandy was born in 1964. The children—Richard was now four, and Patty was a highly active two year old—kept their mother busy. During the next two years Dotty nursed her brood of preschoolers through the normal childhood illnesses. Their only scare was when Richard contracted the measles. Dotty had Patty and Sandy innoculated with gamma globulin to lessen the severity of the measles, and to keep Patty from spiking a fever. Patty successfully passed through the measles without a convulsion.

These thoughts were safely stored, almost forgotten by the time Patty was four and a half. One fresh spring morning Dotty dropped Richard off at school, and the girls and she went to the laundromat. Patty and Sandy dodged and chased each other around the island of washers.

"Sit down; you'll fall and hurt yourselves," Dotty directed, offering them a few toys she'd brought to occupy them. Sandy, a serious two-year-old, played quietly with her stuffed animals, but Patty twisted and squirmed.

"Patty. Settle down!" Dotty urged every few minutes. She noticed Patty seemed distracted, flighty.

Dotty pulled her last load of clothes out of the dryer. "Patty, I'm almost done." She turned to the girls. "Please settle—" Patty was lying on the cement floor; her arms and legs thrashed; her head and body jerked and twitched. Instantly, the old memory flooded over Dotty. She was terrified, but tried not to reveal it. She didn't want to scare Sandy.

"Come on, Sandy." Dotty scooped up Patty and wrestled them into the camper. *Where's a hospital? A doctor's office?* She wondered frantically.

She recognized the gas station where they always traded, and drove to the open door. "I need a doctor—my daughter's having a convulsion!" she blurted to the familiar attendant.

"I'll take you." He quickly jumped in and sped Dotty and the girls to a nearby medical center.

By the time they reached the doctor's office, Patty's convulsion had ceased. The physician who examined Patty said she had had a fever-induced convulsion, but she was fine now. Ascribing no urgency to the situation, he sent them home.

A few months later, when Patty had her third convulsion, their doctor again told them, "Don't be alarmed. Many children have convulsions when they are sick and have fevers."

Although Jim and Dotty were told this repeatedly, they were puzzled. Patty had never shown any signs of a fever or illness before her three convulsions.

Down deep, Jim and Dotty knew something was wrong with Patty, but they never spoke about it. They wanted to believe the doctor when he stated Patty would outgrow these fever-induced convulsions before the age of six. A vague underlying uneasiness lingered, but they tried to tuck it away when all was going well.

Patty was not quite five when she started kindergarten. She greeted school joyously and was easily passed to first grade. She had definite ideas and interests, but a hint of shyness shadowed her spunky, talkative, sanguine spirit.

"Daddy, I want to be a ballerina," six-year-old Patty announced.

"Sure, sweetheart," her father smiled.

"Can I take ballerina lessons?"

"Ask mother. I have to go now. Come on Richard!" Jim yelled. "We'll be late to your game."

Patty stood by the open door and wistfully watched Jim and Richard hurry off to his Little League baseball game. Patty's bangs and boyish haircut framed her elfin face.

"Patty, have you seen Sandy?" Dotty came up behind Patty.

"She's in the bedroom. Mommy, can I be a ballerina?" Patty circled her arms, wobbled on tiptoe for a few steps, then teetered forward and fell on the couch.

"I guess so, if I can find a dance class on a day when I'm not working. Or maybe your father can take you in-between his sales schedule." Dotty talked to Patty as if she understood the details that needed arranging.

Dotty knew Patty needed to develop grace and coordination. Sandy, now four, was able to do things with an efficiency and ease that escaped Patty.

The only class Dotty could find was one that offered tap dancing and acrobatics. Patty's disappointment was soothed by her shiny black dancer's suitcase, matching steel-toed shoes, and leotards. Even though Patty played pretend in her dance costume more than she practiced, she knew her routines by heart.

In July, the studio invited parents to a dance presentation. The evening's festivities were held in a large public auditorium. Under the theme "It's a Small World," thirty-three dance numbers featured tiny tots to teens, with an intermission and grand finale. Patty glowed like a porcelain doll. Her silky peach tights were trimmed in glistening white braid, and huge satin bows were tied at her side and pinned to her hair. She danced with five other girls in two routines.

After the recital, no one said a word to Patty about her bow being askew or her timing and step being slightly offbeat. Sensitive about herself, Patty knew it, and she tucked the memory away in her heart. At home it was still her night to shine. She paraded her costume for Granddad and Grandma Sturgis, who never missed any of their grandchildren's performances. Dotty had decorated a cake to celebrate Patty's dancing debut. Everyone applauded an encore of Patty's favorite "Candy Shoppers" routine.

"This is a happy birthday party!" Patty exclaimed, and clapped her hands with her audience. Then she curtsied and danced her routine again.

The next two and a half years slipped by quickly for Patty. Despite being a highly overactive, busy child, and one of the youngest in her classes, Patty did above-average work in school. By the time she reached third grade, Dotty and Jim were convinced she'd outgrown her fever-induced convulsions and they were again forgotten. Then suddenly, like an earthquake that strikes unexpectedly, Patty had another convulsion. Her class had returned from recess and settled down to read. The children were unusually quiet, absorbed in their stories, when Patty fell out of her chair.

"Look at Patty! She's on the floor!" a boy near her cried out.

Her classmates looked up from their books to see Patty writhing on the floor, her arms and legs jerking and flailing. Her eyes were open, but she was unconscious and the color had drained from her face. The convulsion was over almost as quickly as it began, but the children were screeching hysterically. Patty's body and limbs were limp and still, and saliva drooled from her gaping mouth onto the floor.

The teacher, who had been frantically summoning help, rushed back into the room with the janitor. He scooped Patty up in his arms and carried her to the nurse's office.

By now, Patty had started to come out of her stupor. She was lying on a cot, and all she could think about was how embarrassed she felt. She vaguely remembered the children screaming and running around her, and when her mother came to pick Patty up, she broke down.

"I lost control and wet my pants," she wept as if she were confessing a bad deed she'd committed.

After Patty's teacher calmed the class she tried to explain to the children about Patty's convulsion, but she didn't know the proper terminology. At home the children described Patty's seizure to their parents, who added their misconceptions. None of them anticipated the repercussions: the children became afraid of Patty; they shunned her and wouldn't play with her.

The afternoon Patty had her convulsion, Dotty took her to their family physician. He scheduled Patty for an electroencephalogram (EEG), which records and measures the electrical impulses transmitted by the brain. A week later he advised Dotty, "Patty's brain wave pattern shows that she has a seizure disorder." Then he prescribed phenobarbital to help control Patty's convulsions.

Patty was listening to her mother and the doctor, without understanding what they were talking about or why she would be taking the medicine. She heard her mother say jokingly, "No matter how much medicine you give this girl, she's still going to have too much energy. She's always go-go-go!"

Patty figured the pills had something to do with what had happened to her in class. She thought to herself, *I'll take two or three pills instead of just taking one. That way I'll get rid of this embarrassing thing. It will never happen again and I won't have so much energy.*

One morning after she'd taken the extra pills for several days, she started towards her parents' bedroom. Suddenly, the whole world was spinning around her like a merry-go-round, whirling up, down, and around; brassy music rang in her head, blurred faces and scraps of color whizzed by. She had to pass the stairway, and she thought she was going to fall down the stairs. Her father was doing his sit-ups and she started to stagger around him.

"Patty, if you don't move I'm going to hit you!" her father puffed.

"Daddy, I can't help it." Patty crashed onto the bed.

She lay there until her father ordered, "You'd better get up. You're going to be late for school."

Jim was rushed and didn't notice that Patty was acting unusual. The dizziness had passed enough for Patty to dress herself, and she went off to school without saying anything.

In class, her teacher asked, "Patty would you come up and put the date on the board?"

Halfway through writing the date, Patty felt queasy and dizzy.

Her hand fell, screeching the chalk all the way down the board. She crumpled onto the floor.

This time her teacher kept the class calm, but Patty was out of school for several days. To her child's mind, she thought it was a great vacation. She didn't understand that the medication had to wear off. Unwittingly, Dotty allowed Patty to take her routine dosage. Added to what Patty had in her system, it put her in a stupor. When Dotty took Patty to the doctor the next day, he told them to skip a couple doses until they could regulate the medication.

The day Patty returned to school, her feelings pulled her in two directions. She had always loved school and she wanted to be with her friends. But now she felt uncertain; she had an odd feeling of change and loss. She feared her friends would shy away from her like they had before. It didn't make sense to her. Why were they afraid of her? Because she'd had this strange thing happen to her that she didn't understand?

Patty kept wishing her classmates would forget about it, but they didn't and her isolation intensified. A cold loneliness engulfed Patty. It was hard having to win acceptance and find a place all over again within an established circle of friends.

It dismayed Patty so much that she pleaded with her parents, "Please, don't make me go to school. The children won't play with me."

A hundred protests rose in Jim's and Dotty's hearts. They wanted to rush to school and make the children accept their daughter, but they knew they couldn't. Because of this devastating reaction and the lack of understanding, Jim and Dotty decided to keep Patty's seizure disorder a secret. Although they didn't understand it themselves, they knew it was frightening and unacceptable to society. As long as Patty didn't have another convulsion, they were safe and free to live as if she had never had one. It was easier that way.

As the weeks slipped by, the school situation improved. Patty was friends with Jenny Baker, who was popular, and the children accepted Patty as Jenny's shadow.

Patty's activities helped take her mind off being left out. There were dancing lessons, and public performances and parades with her dance group. She joined Brownies and then Girl Scouts. Richard, Sam, and she played summer league baseball. When Patty turned ten, her father and she started running a mile. Sometimes Patty ran daily, other times she ran only when she felt like it. By the sixth grade, she ran regularly with her father. It was during this time that they acknowledged the reality of Patty's mysterious disorder.

Patty had become lax about taking her medication. It had been so long since her last convulsion that the medication didn't seem to be necessary anymore. To Patty, the memory of her disorder was vague, like a half-remembered nightmare, until she had another seizure in class. This time her sixth grade teacher told her classmates she'd fainted. He picked Patty up and carried her to the office. He tied a ribbon in her hair so she wouldn't get it in her mouth, and turned her on her side so she wouldn't choke. Because he kept the class quiet, they weren't alarmed.

Patty returned to school the next afternoon, because she didn't want to miss a baseball game against a rival team. Her classmates expressed their concern. "How are you? Do you feel all right?"

"Fine," Patty answered shyly.

"Good, we're glad you're back!" the children replied.

It was as if nothing had happened, and Patty was relieved that they were so happy to see her. No one had made a commotion about her convulsion, and Patty thought having another one hadn't been so awful as she had feared.

At the same time, Dotty took comfort in one thought. *At least my daughter doesn't have epilepsy.* Then, when she asked the doctor about getting a medical ID bracelet, he told Dotty not to have the word *epilepsy* engraved on it. Instead, he told her to use the word *seizure.*

"But Patty doesn't have epilepsy, does she?" Dotty asked, astounded.

"Yes, she does," the doctor confirmed.

Until that moment, Dotty had no idea that *seizure disorder* and *epilepsy* meant the same thing. Dotty wasn't sure if she hadn't wanted to hear the word before or if she had just pushed it away. Now that she was finally faced with Patty's epilepsy, she was able to accept it.

In a sense, it was a relief to know something definite. What was clear to Dotty now, and almost too distressing to think about, was the response of others. She wondered, *how will our parents take this news? What will our friends feel about it? Will they understand?*

When Dotty thought about the adverse reaction Patty suffered in third grade, it was still freshly painful. It was this shame and prejudice connected with epilepsy that Dotty feared; and she couldn't stand the thought of having her daughter subjected to it again. The more Dotty reflected on it, the more convinced she was that she must keep Patty's epilepsy hidden. As the months moved by and Patty's life unfolded, Dotty knew she'd made the right decision.

3   *Scrapbook Pieces*

DOTTY unlocked the front door and inhaled the quietness. Theirs was a comfortable, two-story home, rich in warm maple tones. Stepping down into the living room, she set her nursing books on the coffee table, and walked through the dining area into the kitchen. Dotty fixed herself a ham sandwich, wandered into the family room, and collapsed at the dinette. In the corner, an antique rolltop desk yawned with papers and scrapbooks. Two walls of trophies paid tribute to athletic achievements.

She tried to eat her lunch and relax, but cleaning, Thanksgiving preparations, and studies nagged her thoughts. She was enrolled in college, taking a full load to prepare for a career in vocational nursing. She was torn between a multitude of needs and her desire to finish a favorite project. She'd just picked up Patty's thirteenth birthday pictures and wanted to update her scrapbook. There were still a couple quiet hours before her children arrived home from school, so Dotty opted for finishing the scrapbooks and family albums.

It was two-fifteen when Sam came in from school. She was quietly looking at her own scrapbook when Patty tripped into the family room fifteen minutes later, her loose flying hair fell over her shoulders and face. Sam's face was rounder, softer than Patty's. Although Patty was in eighth grade and Sam in fifth, they were about the same height, and they shared the hazel eyes characteristic of the Wilson family.

"Hi, Mom! Hi, Sam!" Patty smiled and plopped her school books on the coffee table. Then she slipped some cookies out of a package on the counter, and poured herself a glass of milk.

Richard shuffled through the front door and into the kitchen right behind Patty. His black hair was short and curly, like his mother's. He had his father's six-foot height, but he was of medium build and gangly, like any other growing ninth-grader.

"How was cross-country practice?" Patty asked. "I'm going out next year!" she announced.

"No, you're not! There's no girls' team. How 'bout pouring me a glass of milk, klutz?" Richard tried to grab a cookie out of Patty's hand.

"You can get your own." Patty flounced by him and sat down at the table next to her mother and Sam.

A hungry bear, Richard rummaged for something to eat, then stretched out across the family room couch to hibernate. He had always been a person of few words. Sam and Richard were close; she was the little sister who could play sports like the guys. Although Patty worshipped Richard, they clashed. He tolerated her and loved her at the same time, but he wasn't about to show anyone how he felt.

"Richard's already sleep," noted Patty as she opened her bulging red scrapbook and started to leaf through it. "You added the pictures from my sixth-grade play," Patty remarked. She stretched across the table and propped her head on her hand so she could see the inscription and read it aloud to her mother and Sam. " 'Wizard of Oz. Afternoon Cast. Witch of the North: Patty Wilson.' Good witch of the north. I hated the costume, and the part wasn't that great either!"

"It was better than being the bad witch, right?" said Dotty.

"Yeah," laughed Patty. "Here's the award I got that night after the play. 'Award for the Outstanding Girl in Mr. Taylor's* Sixth Grade Class.' Remember? Daddy and you couldn't go, so I went with Jenny Baker's family. She was Dorothy. She got to perform for the parents at night, but I didn't. When they gave out the awards, I got second and I got a certificate. And who else but—!"

"Jenny Baker," mumbled Sam.

"Jenny got a trophy," Patty went on. "Everybody was congratulat-

*Name has been changed.

ing her and she was crying and her teacher, Miss Colton,* said, 'Jenny, you had no competition!' And I was standing right there! Then I got in the car with her family and all her brothers and sisters. They go, 'You're the best. No one else was any good.' They went on and on. I was in tears. They forgot I was even in it."

"I know it was hard; the whole neighborhood situation was hard," added Dotty.

Patty paused, then stretched her arms, reflecting. "In sixth grade Carol kind of came between Jenny and me. It was never the same again. I felt left out of our whole block."

"Yes, there were a lot of hurt feelings," agreed Dotty.

"Not because of my seizures; nobody knew about them. I felt left out because Jenny and Carol wouldn't play with me and I wasn't any good in sports. I couldn't keep up with the guys like Sam could. Look, Sam!" Patty exclaimed abruptly. "Here's the picture of us when we were on the Golden Stars baseball team."

"With my broken arm," Sam stated matter-of-factly.

"Yeah, I must have been bad luck for you. They didn't have enough girls for the team, so they asked me to go out. That was crazy! I was a two-inning player out in left field. If you hadn't broken your arm you'd have played catcher for the whole game. You're a great player, Sam! You were always a team leader, too."

"I don't like to get in front of people!" Sam drew back.

"I know, but you're the silent leader. The kids turn to you. They respect you. I was the tag-a-long."

Sam didn't answer; it embarrased her to be talked about. Even though she was extra shy and quiet like Richard, she excelled in sports and scholastics.

"Sam, here's the silly Golden Stars award I got," Patty grinned and chattered on. " 'Be it known,' " she read, " 'by all who are present that on this 30th day of June 1973, Patty Wilson, being more proficient than anyone else at constant mouth motion, is awarded this certificate by order of the Golden Stars.' I wasn't mouthy. I was very very quiet!"

"Sure, sure," giggled Sam.

*Name has been changed.

"I guess I must have done something to get this one. Everybody got an award, and each one said something different. What does yours say, Sam?"

"I don't have one in my scrapbook. I just have a team picture and the Mt. Whitney pictures."

"Oh, yes. Mt. Whitney! That was another one of your father's promotions," sighed Dotty. "He always wanted to climb Mt. Whitney. Remember, we were on our way home from our vacation at Yosemite. We came through Lone Pine past the ranger station, and it was open. That was mistake number one. Your father said, 'Let's just drop in and get the material we need for the next time.' "

"Mistake number two," remarked Sam.

"Then your father said, 'We'll need a wilderness permit if we're going to go up there. Well, let's take one out in case we decide to go sometime.' I should have known!"

"We went to the store and bought beans and Hershey bars and gum and junk to eat," added Patty.

"We didn't have any of the things backpackers have," added Dotty, "like a cook stove. I think we still have those beans around here; nobody could eat them."

"We had to carry those big old heavy sleeping bags," Sam moaned.

"And the ropes cut our sides."

"What's going on?" Jim bellowed. His booming voice woke Richard and startled Dotty and the girls as they hunched over the scrapbook. "Have you girls run today?"

"Not yet." Dotty shook her head.

"We're looking at the Mt. Whitney pictures," answered Patty.

"That was one of the hardest things we ever attempted." Jim pulled his tie off and draped it over the counter, then straddled a kitchen chair on the other side of the table. "Probably the most foolhardy and dangerous."

"Among a long list of others," put in Dotty.

"First of all, we only had tennis shoes instead of hiking boots to hike in, and we didn't know we'd have to walk across the snow," Jim chuckled.

"Slip across the snow."

"And slide."

"It could have been worse. The snow could have broken into an avalanche or we could have fallen in a crevice. We never would have been found. We didn't have any equipment and we carried those sleeping bags that must have weighed twenty-five pounds. None of the new modern ones for us," laughed Jim.

"It rained," Sam muttered.

"It hailed and we had to sit in a cave," commented Dotty. "We didn't know it was the last cave. If we'd have gone farther our gear would have gotten soaked, then we'd really have been in trouble."

"Didn't Patty get sick and throw up? asked Jim.

"She was much better after that," replied Dotty. "None of us felt like eating; we lost our appetite."

"That's the first evidence to me, Patty, that you had lots of guts, when you kept going on." Jim reached across the table and clasped Patty's arm.

"Yeah," giggled Patty. "Richard got sick and he didn't make it, but Sam and I made it to the top."

"I made it to twelve thousand feet!" retorted Richard.

"We just left him at the base camp. I know it's terrible for a mother to leave her son, but I kept thinking Rich would come along. I kept asking people on the trail if they'd seen a boy, but Rich never got very far from the sleeping bag, because he had altitude sickness."

"I thought I was going to die!"

"*We* made it!" teased Patty.

Richard scowled.

"It took Mother to get Sam to go," stated Jim. "She had to count the steps."

"We'd count twenty-five steps and sit down," said Dotty, "twenty-five steps and sit down. And then it got to ten steps and sit down. It was just that bad!"

"Daddy and I went ahead," added Patty. "I tried to keep up with him and I guess he slowed down a little bit for me, but I could handle it. Sam usually outdoes me, but not when we climbed Mt. Whitney."

"When we got back to Richard he was so sick he didn't want to go down the mountain. But I wasn't going to spend another night on that mountain!" exclaimed Dotty. "I've never felt so scared in my life. We had to go down! Rich, you felt better after you reached the lower elevation; you even carried my sleeping bag for me."

"Because you're so slow," remarked Richard.

"It was easy coming down. We ran most of the way," added Sam.

"Mt. McKinley in Alaska may be higher, but you can say you climbed the highest mountain in the continental United States," stated Jim. "I wanted to make it and wanted my family to make it. I wanted you to have the joy of completing something. That's a good feeling! You can look back with pride, just like we are now, for years and years, for the rest of your life, if you finish. But if you don't finish, if you give in, then you've always got it on your mind that you quit or you gave up. I knew I had to be the leader. Even though there was crying, and you were stiff, and you didn't really want to go, I kept pushing. 'Come on fellows. Let's go! You know you can do it.' It was just as hard on me, you know."

"Oh, sure!" the family chorused.

"Then we had this running streak going," Patty said. "We had to run before we left to climb Mt. Whitney, and on the day we got back Daddy made us run in the parking lot. It was hard! We were so tired."

"I haven't missed a day running since January 1, 1971, and your mother hasn't missed a day since New Year's day of 1972. That's been almost four years for me and three for your mother. In fact, I'd better get upstairs and change into my running clothes. Richard, are you going to run with me?" Jim yelled from the top of the stairs.

"I'm going to shoot some baskets." Richard scooped up the basketball and headed out the door through the garage. "Come on, Sam!"

"You know what that means?" said Dotty.

"Daddy will want one of us to run with him," answered Patty.

"I'm playing basketball. See you." Sam scooted out the door.

As Dotty watched Patty lay her head on the table and close her eyes, she recognized Patty's need to reminisce. She was struck with how unlike Patty it was to express hurts and jealousies, to talk about the pain. On the surface, at least, she was positive. She was always cheering the successes of other people, no matter how they treated her. Dotty winced. *I don't think I could return to some of those painful situations with the same enthusiasm. When Jenny moved away I thought things would improve, but life still isn't what it should be for Patty.* Lost in thought, Dotty leafed through Patty's book.

"This was a terrific accomplishment, Patty. Here's your 'Order of The Battered Boot' certificate. April 1974, that was the second time you walked twenty miles for the March of Dimes."

"We just walked it casually." Patty sat up and looked at the award. "It wasn't hard. It was another way I could help; that's why I like to go around and collect for the Jerry Lewis telethon."

"That's true!"

"Oooh, my seventh grade picture. That was awful!"

"It's a nice picture of you, except you could have smiled."

"No! No, I couldn't! Remember, my gums had grown over my teeth and my braces down to here." Patty rubbed the bottom of her top front teeth. "The kids made fun of me. They called me 'Gumby.' My gums are still a little bit puffy, see?"

"It was the Dilantin that made your gums swell, and you aren't taking that medication anymore, so they won't swell again," Dotty assured Patty. "I'm just thankful the oral surgeon was able to remove the extra gum tissue."

"Me too," sighed Patty. "But I've been thinking about something else that's been bothering me. I never remember what happens to me when I have a seizure. You know the one I had in seventh grade?"

"Last January?"

"I guess. It was cold. The one I had when I was sitting in the bean bag chair watching tv. It was different from the one I had in sixth. What happened?"

"I walked past you a couple times and I didn't notice anything was wrong. You know how you scooch down in the bean bag. Then I noticed you weren't watching television. Your eyes had rolled back; I thought you'd had a stroke. I tried to talk to you, but your words were garbled."

"What?" asked Patty.

"Your words didn't make any sense. They weren't even words. They were like tossed salad; you just threw all the letters together and came up with a mixture of words that didn't mean anything. We tried to get you to recognize Sam and Rich and me."

"How did I do on that one?"

"Not very well. You didn't know who we were. We kept holding up the Raggedy Ann dolls to see if you could grasp them, but you sort of batted at them."

"Did you guys laugh or something?"

"No, but you laughed a lot."

"Wasn't it scary?"

"No," answered Dotty, "but there's always a reason to laugh and you were laughing without a reason. I was more concerned you'd had a stroke."

"Did it scare Richard and Sam?"

"They'd never seen you have a seizure before."

"It shook Richard up. He wouldn't start talking to me for a long time. I remember somebody shoving a book in my face and asking me what color it was. I was telling them it was red, and they were telling me it was green. It was a first aid book. I kept saying red, but it was green."

"We were trying to bring you out of it," explained Dotty.

"How'd you know I had a seizure?"

"After half an hour you finally came around and you were fine. You could talk, you were just tired. I looked up *epilepsy* in my nursing book and discovered that you'd had a complex partial seizure. It was the first time you'd ever had that kind. I didn't realize how many kinds of seizures there were. I was so relieved you hadn't had a stroke," sighed Dotty.

"I remember I hadn't run that afternoon and I was going to put my jeans on and Daddy came home. I was running a mile a day. I hadn't broken my streak and Daddy convinced me it wouldn't hurt me to run. 'It won't hurt you!' " Patty boomed, mimicking her father. "So we all went out about 9:30 at night—you and Dad and I—and we ran. It didn't hurt me at all."

"What didn't hurt you?" Jim asked as he charged around the corner into the family room.

"When you made me run that night after my seizure. Everybody thought it would hurt me."

"I wasn't sure myself," Jim said quietly. "Where's Richard? I thought he was going to run with me."

"Sam and he went to play basketball," answered Dotty.

"They gave out on me. How 'bout it Dotty? Patty?"

"I will, Daddy. I have to change." Patty scrambled up the stairs.

"Sam and I will put in our little mile. You know how you are when you run, Jim." Dotty smiled.

"Look's like Patty's the one. She's the only one who didn't desert me."

4 Thirty Miles to Grandmother's House

THE WEEK before the Christmas holiday, a volcano of school problems pushed to the surface and erupted. Once, Patty was sent out of her eighth-grade Spanish class for disrupting it. Another time she told her teacher off and stormed out of the room. During a conference Jim, Dotty, and Patty had with the teacher, Patty silently listened to everything, holding back her words and her emotions. It wasn't until Dotty and Patty were at home in Patty's bedroom that she spewed out her view of the situation.

"Don't believe him, Mom. Believe me! I couldn't say anything in that room, I couldn't! I was so upset."

"You've been having difficulty with several of your teachers," Dotty replied.

Patty pulled herself back on her bed and leaned against the wall. "Just with my art teacher and my English teacher. I was late to class; that's why I got in trouble. My Spanish teacher says I talk a lot. He said I upset his class, but I don't think I do. I don't like him! I don't like anything he does! He gave me tests and I threw them away!"

"There will always be people you don't like, but you'll fail if you don't do your work. Try to get along with your teacher and finish out the year," urged Dotty.

"I wish I were like Sam," Patty spoke wistfully. "She gets along great with her teachers. She's quiet." Patty sat upright. "You know what one of my teachers said to Sam? 'Your sister's a monkey. She's all over the chairs and desks. She never sits still!' I'm not that way in class. I'm not all over the chairs. My teacher said she was in love with Richard. She thinks he's so fantastic, she said, 'Sammy, you have such a wonderful brother!' " Patty mimicked, then slumped into her pillow. "It's kind of sad that I'm the only bratty one, Mom, but usually I get along in school."

"You'll have a breather next week when Christmas vacation starts."

"I'll try harder, Mom. I promise!"

"Are you running with me or not?" Jim peeked his head inside the door.

"Yeah," Patty answered. Running would be their time to talk out the school problem, to work it through, to try to resolve it.

When Jim and Patty returned from running, Dotty, Richard, and Sam were watching television in the family room. "Guess what Patty and I decided to do?" Jim announced. "We're running to Grandmother's house on New Years day."

"But Jim, that's thirty miles away!" cried Dotty.

"Patty couldn't make it around the block," sniped Richard.

"Jim!" gasped Dotty. "What about the time you ran to Bellis Park?"

"What about it?"

"I got a bug in my eye," Patty explained, and Dad said, 'Your eye may hurt and it may be hot, but—"

"—if you're going to become a champion you can't let something like a little bug or heat stop you," finished Jim.

"I'm taking the first shower!" Patty flounced by Richard and they shoved each other in passing.

"You know what I mean, Jim. Patty had a seizure."

"I know; I was there! Don't you think it scared me when Patty turned battleship gray? I had to give her mouth to mouth resuscitation. She talked to me in her lettuce-talk, and walking home she told me, 'I hate you!' I knew she didn't mean it. I thought it was because I'd made her run farther than she'd ever run, and she was upset. I felt terrible! But Dotty, Patty wants to run, and I want her to feel equal to the other kids. When you feel someone isn't equal, like Patty, you can't stand it!"

"And look, Richard!" Jim shouted, smacking his fist against the palm of his hand. "Nobody thinks Patty can do anything! Including me. I always thought she'd be my little ballerina. She'd wear pretty dresses and grow up and bake cookies like grandmother. I've excluded her. It's been father and son everything. You and I walked to the bottom of the Grand Canyon and back, but mother wouldn't let Patty go. If it's a ball game, we go or Sam goes, but not Patty. I'll prove it to all of you. Patty will make it to Grandmother's!"

Richard didn't answer, nor did Dotty. It was impossible to oppose Jim when he was angry, or when he'd set his mind to accomplish a goal.

During ordinary workouts Jim was accustomed to running longer distances, but Patty and Jim only put in a maximum of two to five miles a day to train for their run to Grandmother's.

The weather on December 31, 1974, was ominous: fifty-mile-per-hour winds swept Southern California, and the air was a brisk forty degrees. But on New Year's day the sun was shining and the wind had died down. They'd miss the eighty-sixth annual Rose Parade, but they'd have their own parade, with Patty and Jim running and Sam riding alongside on her bicycle.

Because it was a holiday, the streets were empty and the stores were dark cocoons. To dispel boredom, Patty and Jim explored the roadside while they ran, and Sam scouted ahead of them. There were little things to see and treasures—missed and hidden to the masses scurrying to and fro during the weekday rush—to find. They looked for coins and found mostly pennies.

Jim paused at a newsstand to check the paper. The headlines, which spoke of the continuing Watergate scandal and falling gold prices, put a damper on New Year's high spirits.

At the fifteen-mile mark they had reached Compton and stopped to rest on a curb, when a sheriff's car pulled up beside them. The officer rolled down his window part way and asked, "Did your car break down? Do you need help?"

"No, thanks. We're fine," Jim answered.

"What are you doing in this area?"

"We're running from Orange County, near Knott's Berry Farm, to our grandmother's house in Los Angeles," Jim explained.

"Did you know you're in a dangerous high crime area? If I didn't have my gun and my dog I wouldn't be over here myself. I hope you realize what the hazard is."

"No, sir. We didn't."

"Why don't I give you a ride just to get you out of this area? Then you could continue."

Up to that point, all Jim had been concerned about was making thirty miles. He hadn't realized they might be in a hazardous situation.

"No, we can't," he said, finally. "We have to run it every step of the way."

The officer shook his head, scowled, and left. Jim said, "Come on girls. We better move a little faster."

When they had reached twenty-seven miles, Patty sat down on the steps of a car dealership on Crenshaw Boulevard. A salesman came out and asked what they were doing.

Patty explained to the man, adding, "I can't go any farther." Tears trimmed her eyes.

"How far have you run?" he asked.

"I don't know."

"How many more miles do you have to go?"

"Two or three," muttered Jim.

"I can't do it," wept Patty.

"You're not going to stop now," the salesman said. "You're almost there. If you quit, you'll be sorry. Keep on running; look what you'll accomplish. I don't know any girl your age who's ever run thirty miles."

"I can't finish."

"You can do it. If you've run this far, surely you can run two or three more miles."

Patty wiped the tears from her eyes with the sleeve of her sweatshirt. "Okay, Daddy, let's go."

"That's the spirit!" the man applauded as Patty trotted down the street.

They reached Grandmother's before the Ohio State–USC football game started. It was an exciting game, the kind that usually charged Jim, but instead he was upset and brewing. Patty hadn't received the recognition he felt she deserved. Dotty and her parents were more grateful for the fact that Patty had made it safely, than they were elated she'd run it all the way. They had feared Patty would have a seizure or be injured in an accident, and they didn't want her to try another long run.

It was Richard's off-the-cuff remark—"Patty was just lucky!"— that stoked the fire within Jim.

"I promised Patty I'd make her into a star. I'll make her famous!" he broadcast, emphasizing each word.

Patty was encouraged that she'd made the thirty miles without quitting. She had run a mile every day for three years without breaking her streak, and on the strength of those two successes she decided to join the Patriots, an AAU girls' track team coached by Bob Hickey, a Los Angeles police officer. Every afternoon from four to six-thirty, Patty worked out at Golden West College in Huntington Beach.

On March 22, 1975, Patty and Jim entered the Fifth Annual Los Angeles Marathon. It was raining at the start of the race, but Patty didn't let it hinder her. Her pace was slow and steady.

At the twenty-mile mark Patty "hit the wall." She'd been told the body's energy is exhausted at around that point, and only pure, mental determination could propel a runner past the wall. She wanted to go on, but there was a time limit on the race and she had to stop. This time Patty didn't feel defeated; she knew she'd had the courage to go through it.

In April, she entered an all-comers one-mile run at the University of California's Irvine campus. Her competitors were eighteen years and older. She placed last, but she was pleased and so was her coach; 6:16 was her fastest time yet.

She hadn't won a race on the Patriots track team. Watching her run, Jim felt Patty was trying to train her mind to propel her body faster, fighting the epilepsy medication that programmed her to slow down. It was like trying to drive a race car with the brakes on, but Bob Hickey loved Patty and worked with her as if she were one of his best runners. As the season progressed, there were no firsts or seconds or thirds or even fourths for Patty; she almost always finished last. But, like a true athlete, her determination and enthusiasm kept her going.

Patty may not be fast, but she has endurance. I promised her I could make her a star running long distances, reflected Jim. *And if I can get her picture in the paper, get her some recognition, maybe she'll get along better in school and the girls on the block will accept her. If she can reach a goal she never thought she could reach, she'll gain confidence in herself.*

Jim dreamed of accomplishing a feat worthy of his childhood heroes, Jack Armstrong and Superman. Why couldn't he and Patty run a lot farther than thirty miles? Jim shared these fantasies with Patty when they ran together, or when he drove her home from Patriots practice. They agreed to try a one-hundred-mile run to San Diego in May, and started running thirty to forty miles each week to train for it.

The week before the San Diego run, Jim called the press to announce their plans. In the picture of Patty that soon appeared in the local newspapers, she looked younger than her thirteen years, braces filled her smile. A petite five feet two, she weighed a solid 110 pounds.

In one newspaper article, which portrayed the Wilsons as a warm family and heralded their athletic achievements, Patty had a special announcement. She told the paper, "I'm running in the Palos Verdes marathon in June, and in September I plan to become the first girl on the Buena Park High School cross-country team."

Yet one secret was not shared; the risk was too expensive, the possibility of stigma too severe. Jim feared Patty would be barred from future competition in races and marathons if the press, the public, and her acquaintances discovered that she had epilepsy.

5 San Diego: Trains, Planes, and Marines

THE LAST bell of the day rang, returning Patty's thoughts to something she'd almost forgotten about during school. *Daddy and I start our run to San Diego in a few minutes. How far is a hundred miles? I sure can't measure it. San Diego? That's where we went to the zoo with Grandma and Granddad.* Patty tucked her books in her arms and moved out of the classroom with the other eighth graders. The sidewalks were slick as cellophane from a recent light rain. *Daddy knows where we're going; I'll try my new Spanish words on him, and he'll tell me about his work.*

It was a quarter to five when Grandma and Granddad Sturgis, Richard, and Sam gathered outside the house to watch Dotty take pictures of Jim and Patty. The two were standing on their starting spot: home plate painted in the middle of the street. Jim and Patty were dressed in matching blue silky shorts, baseball caps, and white Los Angeles Marathon T-shirts. Patty performed her warm-up exercises, then Jim and she doffed their caps. Sweeping them gallantly through the air, they bowed goodbye to their family and sprinted out of Redwood Circle.

The streets were clogged with rush-hour traffic; exhaust fumes choked the air. People scurrying down the sidewalks, cars swerving in and out of supermarket driveways, and children whisking down the street on skateboards and bicycles demanded Jim's and Patty's attention. They ran facing traffic in order to watch for oncoming cars —if they ran with the traffic, they would be defenseless against cars pressing in from behind. Even so, the sudden appearance of fast-moving vehicles was a constant threat. When they stopped to cross Valley View, the street was clear; but as Jim jumped over a puddle, a car careened around the corner, frisking his shorts with its fender.

"Daddy!"

"I almost caught him," laughed Jim.

"That car almost hit you!"

"Let's get across this street before another car uses us for target practice."

Nothing can harm my Daddy. He's not afraid of anything.

Jim knew danger was an ever-present, unwelcome running partner, but he suppressed his fears and refused to display them. They headed down Knott, a long thoroughfare dotted with shopping malls, homes, gas stations, and supermarkets. There would be plenty of gas stations to stop at for a drink of water, but few places to rest. When they reached Huntington Beach, they'd run about twelve miles. As the sun set, splashes of pink dressed the wispy clouds and sky. The excitement that had energized them at the beginning started to evaporate, and—oddly—it was Patty who had to spur Jim on. By the time they neared Pacific Coast Highway, the gray darkness was closing in.

"Let's go, Daddy! There's the beach." Patty quickened her pace.

"I hope mother's there; I'm freezing." Jim limped behind Patty. "This damp wind cuts right through you."

"Come on, Daddy!"

"I've had a rough day. I'm tired and sore and I have a blister on my toe."

Patty dashed to the corner of Goldenwest and Pacific Coast Highway. "I don't see the camper."

"I put a dime in my hat. I'll call and see when Mother left home.

"There's a phone booth, Daddy."

"The phone's ripped out!" In frustration, Jim smacked the booth. He surveyed the area, looking for another phone booth, a business or a service station that was still open, but there was nothing. "We'd better wait for her under the light. It's too black on that highway; Mother would never see us." It was an uninviting spot; graffiti had been etched defiantly into the walls of the booth, the phone book hung in limp shreds, and trash littered the dirt around them.

"Do you think Mother's lost?" Jim teased. "We look like a couple of waifs standing out here."

The pungent ocean air chilled Patty. She wrapped her arms around herself and bounced up and down, trying to keep warm. Waiting seemed to last forever.

"Mom! Mom!" Patty and Jim frantically waved at the red camper slowly moving toward them.

"What took you so long?" Jim grumbled, then kissed his wife.

"It took me longer to shop, pack, and fix dinner than I expected," explained Dotty. "I have some hot chicken ready."

"I'm too tired to eat." Jim crawled up in the back of the camper and stretched out on the bunk.

"Me, too," echoed Patty and almost instantly she was sound asleep.

"Wake me up in a half hour. We're behind our twenty-five-miles-a-day average. We'll have to put in a few more miles," Jim told Dotty, and promptly dozed off.

After their nap, Jim and Patty resumed their run. By the time they had run 18.7 miles, it was 8:15. Jim was still too tired to eat, and Patty only wanted a container of yogurt before they went to bed.

Friday morning, May second, Jim and Patty were out running by 6:50. They continued on the Coast Highway through Newport Beach, past businesses and edges of the coastline, over rolling hills into Corona Del Mar. They stopped for a rest on the grassy bluffs. It was a brilliant, cool day; the ocean sparkled in an ever-changing kaliedescope of blues, and sailboats skimmed through Newport Bay past the jetty. Below them, children on a school field trip climbed the rocks to explore the tide pools for sea creatures.

Jim was stretched out on the grass, sleeping. Dotty and Patty were walking Alfred, their German shepherd, when a man and his wife strolled up to them.

"You're that girl, the one in the newspaper!" the man blurted. "I just varnished over you yesterday."

"What?" Patty asked.

"I read the article while I shellacked a table. I'm afraid I painted over your face." The man paused, embarrassed. "I'm sorry!"

"That's okay," giggled Patty.

"How many miles have you run so far?" he asked.

"About thirty-one," answered Dotty.

"Do you think you can run a hundred miles?"

"I wasn't sure until I saw my picture in the paper telling about the run; then I was determined to do it." Patty seized his challenge; she was excited that someone had recognized her. After their break on the bluffs, Jim and Patty completed a 28.9 mile day at San Clemente.

Before attempting the hundred mile run, Jim and Dotty had scouted the entire route and discovered that the only direct road to San Diego was State Route Five, the freeway. Since it's illegal for pedestrians to be on the California freeways, they had to locate connecting side streets and minor highways where Patty and Jim could run. Dead-end streets were another hazard they had to check for and avoid. Halfway to San Diego, Route Five runs through Camp Pendleton, a 125,000-acre Marine base. It is the only public highway to do so. If Patty and Jim were denied freeway access, their only alternatative would be to go around the base to reach San Diego—an added hundred miles—or to use a military road that parallels the freeway. Jim and Dotty had written for permission to run on this military road; all they had to do now was call the main gate and inform them they would be passing through.

When a Marine answered the phone at the main gate, Jim introduced himself and said, "My daughter and I would like to go across the base tomorrow morning at about seven o'clock."

"I'm sorry sir, but we're not allowing anyone on the base," replied the Marine.

"But I have a permit to use the road that the bicyclists use," answered Jim.

"No one is allowed on the base because we're setting up housing for Vietnamese and Cambodian refugees."

"My thirteen-year-old daughter and I have fun fifty miles from our home in La Palma to San Clemente. We're halfway to San Diego. Isn't there some way we could get special permission?"

"Only military personnel are allowed on base, due to the tight security," the Marine answered.

"Do you mean to tell me there's no way?"

"You could run a hundred miles around the base."

"We're only running a hundred miles total. You wouldn't want to disappoint a little girl who's run all this way, would you? Her picture was in the paper announcing to the world she was running to San Diego. Couldn't you ask a senior officer?"

"No, sir," the Marine said with finality. "The base is strictly off-limits!"

Daily transport planes had just delivered the first of over eighteen thousand Vietnamese and Cambodian refugees expected in Southern California. It would become the largest and longest emergency airlift of human beings in history. To prepare for the refugees, Camp Pendleton personnel had worked through the night to set up accomodations in barracks and quonset huts. Ninety big squad tents had also been erected, making a tent city less than five miles from President Richard Nixon's estate at San Clemente.*

Defeat seemed inevitable, but Jim decided to try one last ploy—he called officials in San Clemente to see if they could assist in some way. Jim detailed his and Patty's mission, adding that they'd have to turn back if they couldn't find a way.

"You'd be arrested by the Highway Patrol if you even try to run on the freeway," the man told him. "Unofficially, the only thing I can suggest—and I'll totally deny I told you if you're caught—is to go down near President Nixon's estate and run along the railroad tracks that go right through the base."

"How far is it?" Jim asked.

"It's about twenty-two miles from San Clemente to Oceanside. Good luck!"

Patty awoke to a steel black morning. Still half asleep, she did her regular routine of exercises to limber up. They made her hungry, but she knew she wouldn't be eating breakfast; they never ate before

*Information taken from an article by Richard West, *The Los Angeles Times,* 30 April 1975.

running. She sipped some juice, then crawled out of the camper. Pregnant air swaddled her in its watery womb, saturating her sweatshirt, her shorts, and her legs, which were covered with white knee socks. She shivered and tied her waist-length hair into a pony tail intently watching her parents.

"Dotty, stay at the state park at San Clemente until nine o'clock," Jim rehearsed. "That way we can tell the authorities where you are if we get caught."

Dotty nodded. *Try to run another time, when its safe,* she wanted to say. She knew Jim. He'd never quit; he had to make this run for Patty and for himself.

"We should make it to Oceanside before noon. If we don't, we're either lost or in jail."

"Come on, Daddy, let's go." Patty poked her head under Jim's arm and kissed her mother.

"Don't worry, they won't arrest me with this cute little girl at my side," Jim quipped, trying to lighten Dotty's mood as he hugged her goodbye.

Jim and Patty jogged across the sand and stopped momentarily at the railroad tracks to wave to Dotty. Two saucered lights sat high on poles, glaring defiantly into the dark. Patty stared back, refusing to be afraid, and darted down the beach. Ocean breakers rhythmically cannoned their warning, and a white sign pocked with rusty holes silently cautioned, "Trespassing-Loitering Forbidden By Law."

Patty and Jim half-hobbled and half-galloped over the xylophone planks of the railroad tracks. Darkness, rocks, driftwood, and debris demanded their constant attention. A piece of steel peeking up between the ties tripped Patty, and she spilled headlong into the sand and gravel. Jim glanced back to see her sprawled on the ground, and rushed over to see if she'd been hurt.

"Are you all right?"

"I'm fine, Daddy. How far is it to President Nixon's house?" Patty brushed off both the sand and her fall with the same lightness.

"I don't know. It shouldn't be too far."

"Do you think he's at home?"

"I hope not! The secret service will be there if he is. Remember, even if we make it past President Nixon's without being stopped, we still have to cross Camp Pendleton."

A bluff, etched and eroded, jutted to their left. Homes rested on top of the bluff and flights of stairs climbed down the side, abruptly ending behind closed gates. On the other side of the tracks, there was a private beach. A rotating signal light sat on the tip of the bluff to warn approaching aircraft. The train tracks stretched out across the bridge. Underneath, a wide creek quietly quenched the ocean's thirst, while sleepy birds sat undisturbed on the water.

Jim and Patty ran along a narrow ledge instead of on the tracks; black grease smothered the steel wall and railing. When they reached the end of the bridge they slid down under the pillars for a quick break. They knew they wouldn't be spotted and Jim was relieved; they'd made it past President Nixon's estate.

Jim yearned to run on a road, but they couldn't. Rivers and ravines made the beach impassable and the sand was too soft. Alongside the tracks, the slippery gravel, as it flicked up and nicked their legs, was like broken marbles. It seemed they were tied to the tracks. The dampness chilled Patty and Jim and they had no idea where they were or how far it was to Camp Pendleton. A ghostly fog danced around what appeared to Patty to be an old metal factory.

"It's eerie," she shivered. A profusion of lights shone directly on her, tracing her footsteps. Silhouettes of an enormous cement dome and other dinosaur structures could be seen through the misty gauze.

"Look at the lights," Patty called to her father, now a half block ahead of her. "They're scary!"

Jim stopped and waited for her. "They're security lights," he explained.

"What are those things?"

"I don't know, but they don't look friendly." Suddenly a six foot fence crowned with ribbons of barbed wire stood beside them. They quickened their pace. Every fifteen feet or less, signs warned, "Trespassing-Loitering Forbidden by Law. Electric Generating Plant—Receiving Station on Federal Land."

They were passing precariously close to the containment dome and construction cranes at the San Onofre Nuclear Generating Station. In a few minutes they passed the nuclear power plant, and the tracks veered above San Onofre State park, where tents and trailers were parked. Jim and Patty scrambled down to the road that cut through the park and ran as far from the campers as they could. They hadn't eaten and the beachy smell mingled with the aroma of coffee and the hickory of ham and bacon made them hungry. The day was a silky gray by the time they reached the end of the campground. A six foot chain link fence, patchworked with signs and red reflectors, barred their entrance to Camp Pendleton.

"Look Daddy! Look what this sign says!" Patty exclaimed. "National defense installation." Patty read aloud." 'Whoever enters Camp Pendleton for any purpose prohibited by law or regulation will be subject to federal prosecution. No trespassing—enter with permission only.' And look at the big green one behind the fence."

"U.S. government property," Jim read. "Trespassers will be prosecuted under federal and state law."

"We can't go in there, Daddy! We'll be breaking the law."

"Don't worry. I'll lose my job; you won't," laughed Jim. "You won't go to jail; I will. Besides," he spoke soberly, "we have to go through there to get to Mother and she's probably so worried she's biting her nails."

Jim studied the desolate military road and decided it was safe to try the tracks, so they crossed down a small ravine and clambered up onto the ties. It was lighter now; the sun was slowly shooing the fog away. Small companions, squirrels and lizards, dashed and slithered from the sound of people. The tracks still demanded Jim's and Patty's attention; there was no predictable rhythm to the ties. The distance between them varied; some were buried in the dirt while others were not. Jim cocked his head to the side so he could talk to Patty. He didn't know why, but he felt the urge to look up.

"Jump! *Jump!*" he screamed, yanking Patty by the arm. He threw his body over hers and hung on to a flimsy, stickery tumbleweed. Patty clenched a wisp of grass on the shallow embankment. A train cycloned by, sucking them toward its wheels.

When it passed, Jim sat up. He could hear his heart thudding loudly. "You okay, Patty?"

"Sure"

"I was so worried about someone spotting us, I forgot trains run on tracks. Let's take a break." He leaned against the ground as an icy shiver ran through him. He could feel the color draining from his face, and he gazed at Patty, who was sheet white.

Jim wanted to rest, but he didn't dare; he had to get to Dotty. He continued his run with a new rhythm: leap two or three steps, stop to look up for a train, look down at his feet, gallop a step or two, and look up for a train.

Half an hour later, there were still no signs of Vietnamese refugees or Marines. It was an expansive, warm land; shades of green sprayed the scrubby brush and yellow touched the wild flowers. The train tracks, now about a half mile inland, hugged the softly contoured land; they dallied through shallow gulleys, skimmed along flatland, or lumbered up beside a ravine. Ginger hills lay to their left, and the freeway snaked close at times, then slithered away.

Jim started to relax and joke with Patty as he normally did. They made bets about whether they'd get caught. Would they be beaten? How many years would they spend in prison?

As Jim glanced over his shoulder to prod Patty he saw to his horror that no more than a couple hundred yards behind Patty was another train.

"*A train!*" he screamed. Patty and he met in mid-air and flattened their bodies against a slope. The Amtrack train whisked by like a jet. Jim leaned against the dirt and closed his eyes. A vision of two bay-windowed eyes, a blinding headlight, and a red and blue striped silver-needle train appeared and disappeared like a crazy movie flashing back and forth on the screen.

"I didn't hear it coming," Patty whispered, almost inaudibly.

"That train didn't get us the first time; so he thought he'd come back and try again," quipped Jim. "Out here in the middle of nowhere the train was going so fast it wouldn't even know it had hit us. We can't let trains stop us, Patty. We have to get to Mother."

Why am I doing this? Jim chastised himself as they continued down the tracks. *I'm risking my daughter's life for a stupid hundred-mile run. We could have run a hundred miles in any other direction, but no, I have to pick a place where it's against the law to run. The Marines will capture us next; they'll shoot first and ask questions later. I'll lose my job, because I'm bonded, and my wife won't have a husband anymore.*

Dotty had no way of researching the territory; she could only pray the twenty-two miles of track would deposit Jim and Patty in Oceanside as her map showed. She doused her fears in cup after cup of black coffee, called home several times, walked Alfred, and drove down the southbound lane of the freeway hoping to spot Jim and Patty.

She pulled in at the rest stop, and she scanned every section of the tracks through binoculars, but didn't spot them. Time seemed suspended. Finally, Dotty drove on to Oceanside to wait; she didn't realize she had probably just missed Jim and Patty as they followed the tracks under the freeway and out of her line of sight.

Look at the feet. Look out for Marines. Look up and behind for trains. Run forward. "Come on, Patty!" *Look down. Up. Behind. Forward.* "Hurry up, Patty." Jim could almost sing this loony running rhythm out loud. Their knees ached from the jolting gait. Patty's ankle throbbed; she had fallen and twisted it several times. Their throats were parched and they yearned for water and safety.

"Daddy! There's the rest stop. Maybe Mom's there." Patty pointed.

Patty and Jim scrambled down the gorge, then up the hill to the boundary fence. Jim boosted Patty over the chain link fence, then climbed over himself. They hoped a motorist could give them their bearings, but when they came out of the restroom a Highway Patrol car sat facing the spot where they needed to climb back over the fence. Jim sauntered over to the car window and asked the patrolman, "Sir, how far is it to Oceanside?"

"About seven miles," he answered.

Jim wanted to ask, "How long are you going to sit here?" but he didn't. Instead Patty and he sat on the grass a few feet behind the patrol car, and waited for him to leave.

"He thinks we belong to one of the cars at the rest stop," whispered Patty.

"How long is he going to stay there?" grumbled Jim.

"Maybe he's taking a break."

"He's probably waiting to nab a speeder. Pretty sneaky, hiding up here."

"I'll bet Mom's worried."

"She'll have an ulcer if we don't get out of here. If we could only contact her! What are we going to do, Patty?"

They stared back and forth between the fence and the patrol car, but it didn't budge.

"Come on, speeder," laughed Jim. "You'd think we were in East Berlin. There's the policeman. There's the wall. On the other side is freedom."

Patty slumped down and laid face down on the grass. *I wonder where Mom is? I'd feel better if I could see her. Where does Camp Pendleton end? What difference does it make? Can't we get to Mom?*

"Patty, don't be discouraged. We won't quit, no matter what!" Jim punched the air with his fist.

"Sure, Daddy."

"Nothing will stop us. The patrolman will leave any minute now."

Just then, a trail of military jeeps pulled into the rest stop. "Come on, Patty, let's get out of here. We'll crawl behind those bushes and see if we can dig under the fence."

Patty and Jim crept along the fence, camouflaged by large bushes, until they found a small hole. It wasn't large enough, so they used their fingers to try to scratch out the dirt. The hard cement-like clay cut into their hands, but they dug until they burrowed a hole barely large enough to let them crawl through.

Jim pulled the chain link fence, curling it up. "Patty, scoot underneath."

"Daddy!"

"Shhh! Someone will hear us."

"But my pants are caught; they're ripping."

Jim unhooked Patty's pants from the fence and dragged his massive frame underneath. They stole down the ravine and back onto the tracks where they'd stopped. They were in clear view of the rest stop, just a few hundred yards away.

"Run hunched down, so they won't see us," whispered Jim.

"My dad's part Indian, and he's doing his Indian dance," snickered Patty. She resisted the temptation to put her hand over her mouth and give out a war whoop. She knew he wasn't joking; she'd never seen him this scared.

They barely made it past the rest stop when they spotted something Jim hadn't expected to encounter—danger from the sky. A military helicopter hovered in the distance, then dipped down toward Jim and Patty.

"Hit the dirt!" Jim yelled. "Don't move. Act like you're dead."

"They don't care about us."

"We don't belong here, Patty. We're civilians; this isn't some war movie we're reenacting."

When the helicopter finally moved on, they stood to brush themselves off. Having narrowly escaped two trains, crawled under a fence, and ducked a helicopter, they looked like war refugees themselves.

The tracks continued to run along the northbound lane of the freeway, and Jim and Patty had to keep dodging the airplanes and helicopters that circled above them. Without warning, the tracks ran on top of an island surrounded by two rivers of traffic, the north and southbound lanes of the freeway. Motorists, unaccustomed to seeing two people running on the railroad tracks, honked their horns and waved.

Although Jim could laugh about it later, cold fear possessed him. *Watch the tracks, look up, look behind,* he chanted silently. "Hurry up, Patty!" *Look around for Marines. Skip a step. Look up for planes and on both sides of the freeway for Highway Patrol.* Jim knew they had to be close to the main gate, when the tracks unexpectedly forked in two directions.

"Should we go to the left or right?" Jim and Patty asked each other. Because they didn't have a map, they didn't know that one track would lead them along the Santa Margarita river deep into Camp Pendleton, and the other track would lead them to Dotty. They scouted the area, searching for a sign pointing to Oceanside.

"There it is," exclaimed Jim, " 'Camp Pendleton, one mile.' " Pure adrenalin mixed with joy charged their exhausted bodies, aching knees, and blistered feet down the track. Jim abandoned his concern for trains, planes, and Marines. "Just get to Mother!"

About five hundred yards away, Jim sighted an overpass. To their right, behind a fence, a military policeman was sitting in his jeep. Jim saw the oscillating red light on top of the jeep go on just as he spotted Dotty standing on the overpass.

"If you've ever run in your life, run, Patty, Run! Faster! I don't care if your ankle hurts. Forget everything, We have to get to Mother before that MP gets to us."

Jim could see the jeep heading straight toward them, but a cage-like fence stood between them, and the MP would have to work the jeep around it. They ran down a culvert, past a drain pipe, then clawed and dug their way feverishly up the steep embankment to the overpass.

They dashed across the street and dove into the camper. "Go!" Jim shouted to Dotty. "I don't care where. Just get us out of here." Dotty drove out of Oceanside down to Carlsbad. Jim feared they'd be hunted by the Oceanside or military police, but after breakfast and a long nap they were able to laugh as they dramatized their harrowing adventure for Dotty.

After a safe amount of time, they returned to the overpass. One of Jim's unbreakable rules was, "We don't skip anything. We start where we left off. We cover every inch of the ground."

Dotty left Jim and Patty, then drove ahead to reserve a campsite near Cardiff-by-the-Sea. Ordinarily, she drove only a few miles ahead, acting as the statistician, recording the number of miles they ran by clocking their mileage on the truck's odometer. She kept track of hours and the exact location where they started and stopped. She prepared juices for Jim and Patty to drink during their breaks, and one large starchy meal, which was ordinarily the only food they ate after finishing a day's run. Mostly, Dotty and Alfred waited.

It was typical of Southern California that the morning had been a cold, dull gray. Now the afternoon was gold, the sun brilliant, and to Patty the heat was sickening. She had a headache, so Jim asked a sheriff parked by the road if he would let her have a couple of asprins.

"Legally, I can't," he replied, "unless I throw them on the

ground. If you want, you can pick them up and dust them off."

"No, thanks. I'll pass," answered Patty. "I don't need them that bad." But she did. The aftershock from the morning's stress combined with the heat was too much. They stopped north of Leucadia after they'd clocked ten more miles; it had been tough and treacherous, a long thirty-two mile day.

Sunday morning Patty and Jim started at 5:45. Compared to yesterday, it was a tame but not uneventful or easy 20.4-mile day. Climbing the Torrey Pines grade was like running straight up a playground slide. At the University of California, San Diego, Dotty and Jim and Patty lost each other. Dotty went one way around the roads that circle the campus, while Jim and Patty ran another route. They played hide-and-seek, just missing and criss-crossing each other's path. Once Jim and Patty spotted the camper, but Dotty didn't see them. Finally, joyously, they met, and Jim and Patty started toward the finish line at Genesee Avenue and Governor Drive, just outside the San Diego city limits. Dotty had lipsticked *The End—Finish* on cardboards and tacked them onto the tail of the camper to spur Patty and Jim on.

Patty half danced and ran down the road to touch the camper. "Daddy, we made it!"

Jim sat on the back of the camper, his face unshaven, stubbled, and creased. His arms hung limply between his knees. He simply could not respond to Patty.

"How come Daddy's not happy?" Patty asked her mother. "Is he mad? We made it!"

Jim's enthusiasm had been depleted by exhaustion and the shock of all they'd escaped and conquered. The run had been a lark for Patty; she couldn't comprehend why Jim had been robbed of his joy, and she was upset that he wasn't excited.

After a rest, they ate some yogurt—Patty's favorite—and started for home. They stopped at the northbound rest stop just to show Dotty where they'd climbed the fence.

As they looked out across to the tracks and down the canyon to the ocean, they saw a swarm of camouflaged Marines. Their guns and artillery were aimed seaward. The Marines of the Fifth Amphibious Brigade had staged the code name "Bell-Buster" war games. The *USS New Orleans,* the *USS Fresno,* helicopter landing ships, and six troop-carrying ships of the Navy Amphibious Squadron were anchored offshore. The mammoth jaws of amphibious tractors delivered troops, trucks, and tanks. The Marines stormed ashore to assault the "enemy" trenched on the tracks.

All that was missing was a film crew and cameras, but the actors were there, one thousand Marines on land, while ten thousand more manned ships, planes, and helicopters. As Jim listened to the "Boom! Boom! Boom!" of cannons saluting the air, and watched the panorama of Marines hovering above them in helicopters, swarming like ants over the railroad tracks and charging up the beach, he felt he was dreaming. *If we had run today, instead of yesterday,* he repeated to himself, *we'd have run into this mock war.* All he wanted to think about was getting home to Richard and Sam.

Aim for a Star

Aim for a star! Never be satisfied
With a life that is less than the best,
Failure lies only in not having tried—
In keeping the soul suppressed.

Aim for a star! Look up and away,
And follow its beckoning beam.
Make each Tomorrow a better Today—
And don't be afraid to dream.

Aim for a star, and keep your sights high!
With a heartful of faith within,
Your feet on the ground,
and your eyes on the sky,
Some day you are bound to win!

"PLEASE keep this poem and listen to what its saying. We believe you can do it," Dotty wrote at the bottom of Patty's eighth grade graduation card.

Dotty was the celebrator; she applauded her family's accomplishments with festivals, and Patty's graduation was no exception. But then, it was Jim who produced and directed starmaking, life-marking achievements to celebrate. On Flag Day, three days after Patty's junior high school graduation, Jim, Richard, and Patty competed in the Palos Verdes Marathon.

The regal Palos Verdes peninsula presides over an ocean-

*Helen Lowrie Marshall, *Aim for a Star* (Garden City, N.Y.: Doubleday, 1964), p. 7.

engraved shoreline. Its ragged walls cut off the sandswept beaches of the California coastline, and roads are scribbled across its wrinkled terrain. The marathon was advertised as "the most scenic run in the world."

At the starting line, Patty was engulfed by the runners. This would be Jim and Richard's race; theirs was a continuing father-son rivalry. Jim's bywords were, "Hey, Richard! I challenge you to—." Or, "I can beat you at—." Richard, himself a fierce competitor, thrived on his father's challenges.

At the thirteen-mile mark, Jim was exhilerated. He'd passed Richard, and Richard had seen him go by. Then, suddenly, Jim developed a blood blister. He stopped, sat down, and removed his shoe. Richard caught up to him and in passing, shouted, "Hey Dad, why are you stopping?"

Jim had erected a Dad-cannot-quit, Dad-is-invincible image. If Dad is sick, if Dad is dying, if Dad is injured, he will not stop because quitting is failure. If Dad quits, then his children will quit. But now, Dad was sitting with his shoe in his hand.

"I'll pass you again!" Jim yelled after his fleeting son.

But he didn't. He was forced to stop because of the blister. Jim chastised himself, *Why did I quit? Why did I quit? I shouldn't have quit!*

Patty was plodding way behind; Richard was running with the middle group of marathoners. To track the runners, Dotty and Sam drove up and down the route. They picked Jim up and when they drove by Richard, Jim ducked so Richard wouldn't know he'd quit.

"Hey, Rich! Keep going!" Dotty and Sam yelled from the car window.

"How's Dad?" Richard asked.

"He's coming along," answered Dotty.

There was one point where Patty could take a short cut, and she did: her knees were giving out on her. At the twenty-mile mark that nagging shrew, knee pain, forced her to give up.

At the twenty-one-mile mark, Richard's foes became the clock and an exhausted body that wanted only to quit. Even his hair was frazzled, and his fight for oxygen contorted his mouth. But his family was a family that gave the finest gift of all: the gift of self. Nothing was withheld, despite their own exhaustion or defeat; they knew success was rarely achieved without some kind of pain, without effort beyond one's abilities, without the support of a team.

Sam handed Richard cups of water and orange wedges to take the edge off his thirst. Patty and Dotty followed on the sidelines, urging him forward with their cheers. Jim limped behind Richard, talking him through the last five miles.

It was a high for Richard—the first marathon he'd ever finished. He was so proud that he wore his finishers T-shirt until it was too tattered to be worn.

A week later, Patty competed in a one-mile race at the Watts games in Los Angeles. Patty's kick was too high; and when she shot out, her foot hit a girl who fell into someone else—girls tumbled like dominoes. In the stands, Jim and Dotty thought Patty would fall too, but she didn't.

First, second and, third runners crossed the finish. Patty was pressing for fourth when a girl started passing on her right. Patty accelerated to squeeze across the line to win fourth. Fourth place! It was the best she'd ever run, but Patty's elation was temporary. She milled among the other girls the way runners do when they cool down their energy flow, stopping to apologize to the ones who had fallen. She began to feel awful! She persuaded herself that if those girls had run, she wouldn't have placed fourth. How would she have placed? Last?

The goals Jim had dreamed of for Patty—making her mark in running and receiving recognition—had eluded her. He wrote to *Runner's World* to find out what the long distance running record was for a woman, and they informed him that the womens' ultramarathon record was one hundred miles. Patty would have broken that record had she run a couple miles farther on their San Diego run.

"Let's run to Las Vegas. It's glamorous!" Patty suggested, having no idea how far it was to the all-night glitter city.

"We could run during Christmas vacation!" Jim enthused.

"Great!" Patty sealed their agreement.

In September, when Patty entered Buena Park High School, she had the first-week jitters common to most freshmen; yet she joined the school activities with enthusiasm. She tried out for cheerleader so she could yell for all of Richard's games. The previous year he'd received trophies for being the most valuable freshman cross-country runner and basketball player.

There was not a seed of envy in her; there never had been. She worshipped Richard, even though he'd excluded her from street sports. She wanted to participate in his sports successes, and she could if she were elected to the cheerleading squad.

Every day after school, she and her friends practiced the routine they planned to perform at tryouts. The other girls' precision movements accentuated Patty's clumsiness. She felt the definable difference, but making cheerleader consumed her and she was unable to acknowledge it.

She convinced herself that her bubbliness and excitement would help her win. But before the final notice was given, she sensed she hadn't been selected. She filed away her disappointment in her folder of expectations. She'd make it as a sophomore! She'd work harder. She was just as good as her friends who were selected. More practice—that's all she needed.

When cross-country season opened, Patty and a handful of other girls tried out for the team. Compared to the Patriots' training sessions, the girls' workouts were too easy, so Patty trained with the boys. Because there wasn't enough competition in the league for female teams, Patty decided to run with and against the guys. There would be problems, like not being able to take a shower after a meet, because the girls' gym was usually locked. Then, too, the team meetings were held in the boys' locker room.

Even before Patty tried out for cross-country, she had been apprehensive; the coach had read about her San Diego run and seen the accompanying picture of Patty wearing her Patriots shirt. He used Patty as an example to the guys the year before. Richard had been his number one freshman runner. Now she feared·the coach would expect her to have the same quick blood. She wasn't fast and she worried that he'd be disappointed in her. When Richard told her that they were only letting her run with the boys to use her for a psych-out—"No guy wants a girl to beat him!"—she fiercely determined to prove herself.

During the first preseason cross-country event in La Mirada, Patty placed ninth despite her seizure. By the end of the season, she had crossed the finish line ahead of many of the boys, who were embarrased that a girl defeated them.

On November 8th, Patty went to a girls' cross-country invitational in Santa Barbara. Jim and Dotty let her go, even though her family couldn't be there; and she missed the warm feeling of having them cheer for her. Because there were only junior varsity and varsity classifications, Patty had to run JV instead of against freshmen. The unfamiliar two-mile course was hilly and she wasn't able to walk the course in advance.

When Patty flew out of the starting line, she was shocked to realize that she was the front runner. She'd never been out front in her life. It alarmed her. *Oh no,* she thought, *I'll just die! How can I stay up here?* She could hear her father's voice yelling for her, even though he wasn't there. That was even more frightening.

The crowd was screaming, "Patty!" She couldn't comprehend why, but every time they yelled, "Patty! Patty!" it excited her and she ran faster. She was so fired up that she passed the gate she was supposed to turn into, but she'd come in first. She'd won! She'd won her first race!

Then Patty found out that the girl right behind her was also named Patty. Patty had won the race because of the enthusiastic cheering of the other Patty's supporters. Patty had run her first mile in 6:18, and her second mile in 6:49 for a 12:67 finish. She received a medal and plaque that would be displayed prominently on the family trophy shelf. None of the guys from the team had been there to see her win, either, but this race would become one of her favorite highs in her competitive running career.

Patty placed in the upper half of all freshman boys in league finals, and her fastest mile time was 5:53. Richard's sophmore team was

Patty and Jim on a lonely stretch of the 1310 mile trek from Buena Park, California, to Portland, Oregon, in July, 1977. Patty broke her own long distance record on this run.

(Photo courtesy The World, *Coos Bay, Oregon)*

Patty and Pete Strudwick, the footless runner who was an inspiration to Patty throughout her marathons. (Photo courtesy Jim Wilson)

A playful moment during Patty and Jim's hundred mile run from La Palma to San Diego in May, 1975. (Photo courtesy Dotty Wilson)

Henry Winkler and Patty meet while making a television spot about epilepsy for the Epilepsy Foundation of America.

(Photo courtesy EFA)

George Nock, of the Washington Redskins, presents Patty with a plaque on behalf of the Redskins '72 football team.

(Photo courtesy EFA)

(Photo courtesy EFA)

nine-to-zero to win the league championship. At the awards banquet, Patty received a trophy for being the most inspirational freshman runner.

When Patty had picked Las Vegas as their next major run, she didn't know it was three hundred miles. Jim knew it took an hour to fly to Las Vegas and six hours to drive there, but it wasn't until he researched their trip that he discovered that the route was neither "glamorous" nor easy. The majority of the trip would take them across the desert and through Cajon Pass, which peaked at 4,190 feet, and Mountain Pass, 4,276 feet. They'd have to run on perilous stretches of freeway where there were no alternate routes.

The Department of Transportation gave them permission to run on the bicyclists' trails, and Jim used bicycle maps to chart their course. When they scouted a portion of the route a month before the run, a resident of Cajon Pass informed Jim that the temperature rarely dropped below zero in December.

"Zero?" Jim asked. "We've never run in below-freezing weather! Is it normally that cold?"

"It's our usual December temperature," the man answered.

Richard Beard, transportation information officer in San Bernardino, arranged for a permit to run on the freeway, which Jim was to have with him all the time. Mr. Beard also wrote them a letter with additional information:

It occurred to me after your visit to this office yesterday that I had overlooked an important point, namely the possibility of ice, landslides, etc.

The alternate routes such as old Cajon Boulevard are maintained by the County of San Bernardino. Because of restricted funding levels this year at the county level, these roads may not be maintained well, if at all, in some locations.

I spoke with our Deputy District Director to see whether or not we could issue a special permit to use the freeway, in case you became blocked while using an alternate route. He informed me that this would be inappropriate, primarily for safety reasons both for yourself as well as for the motoring public. If conditions are such that the alternates are closed, then we could expect freeway traffic to be extra hazardous, also.

Sorry that we can't get you through this possible hurdle, Jim. You might start now to practice running with snowshoes on. The first snowfall last year was on December 31 in Cajon Pass. Temperatures were in the low forties during the warmest part of the day throughout the week.

During November and December, Jim and Patty ran an average of six miles in the crisp early morning hours to simulate cold weather conditions. On the weekend they ran fifteen to twenty miles a day to train for the thirty-mile day they planned to average on their run.

Jim contacted several newspapers in late November; he gloried in publicizing Patty. Even though he planned to run every mile she ran, he never talked about the Las Vegas run in relation to himself. Patty's acclaim fed his need for recognition. Like an actor on stage, Jim was depressed before an empty theater, alive before an audience. He entertained others with Patty's proposed adventures.

When Jim turns his face a certain way, he has Charlie Brown's profile. He shares some of Charlie's whimsical qualities, too, always hoping to receive his first valentine. Cliff-hangers, feats like running up a mountain through snow or running on a freeway, draw out his daring Jack Armstrong. Yet, anticipating the criticism of outsiders, he'd voice their unexpressed thoughts: "I'm probably the meanest father in the world to make my kid run on Christmas."

Complex, with an almost frightening combination of child and adult, Jim is philosophical and has an uncanny ability to see and touch the heart of life. He has a compulsion to inspire people to try things they'd ordinarily never dare to attempt, then give himself unreservedly to see them succeed. Because of his innate understanding of his family—of their individual frailties and abilities—he recognized that neither Richard nor Sam had the desire, tenacity, or endurance to run ultra-marathon distances. Yet he always attended and applauded their athletic efforts and school involvements.

When Jim talked to the press about their Las Vegas run, he included Richard and Sam, proudly mentioning that Richard had twice received most valuable player and was an All Star baseball player. He pointed out Sam's prowess in catching and noted that she had been chosen to play on the All Star softball team. Jim contrasted their natural ability to Patty's "two left feet" and the way she'd learned to compete. He mentioned the race where Patty finished unconscious, but never explained why. The word epilepsy was never spoken; it was still safely deposited.

Jim told reporters about the road and weather hazards and of their future plans. Patty and he were considering running five hundred miles to San Francisco, he enthused, "then maybe Canada-to-Mexico, and possibly she will be the first female to run across the nation."

Patty wanted to run to Las Vegas, but the publicity wilted her. "Do I have to have my picture taken? Do I have to talk to them?"

Beneath her unassuming appearance, her shyness, and dislike for publicity, she possessed a spirit of steel. When the guys on the cross-country team read the news stories promoting her run, they joked about it and told her a girl could never run three hundred miles. The macho matadors swished their capes, daring Patty to charge. She was feisty, a fighter, determined to win, to rip their smugness to shreds.

Most of the news articles depicted Patty as shy and overshadowed by her father's enthusiasm. Charles Gould, an Orange County journalist did see Patty's spirit, and exposed her feminist views:

> In the everyday war for equality, most women use the law to put their message across, but Patty Wilson uses her legs.
>
> Since January 1, they've carried her about 2,600 miles, but she set herself a 1975 goal of 3,000 miles. So on December 20 she'll stretch it out by running to Las Vegas.
>
> Equality's the reason for the Vegas sprint, says the Buena Park High School freshman who turned fourteen last month. She figures it'll be a big step for women, but particularly women athletes.
>
> "They're not taken very seriously," she claims.*

*Charles Gould, *The* [Orange County] *Register,* 14 December 1975.

7 *The Old Spanish Trail*

THE WEEK before Christmas, newspapers filled their pages with the customary touching stories of children who would have a bleak Christmas without the world's generosity, the whimsical, humorous, and ancient reminders of Christmas' beginnings, and a very special headline: "All she wants for Christmas is a national record." Patty's journey would take her across a desert in search of a long distance running record. She would not be able to reach her destination until after the anniversary of Christ's birth. And she hoped to be there in time to welcome in another birthday celebration—America's bicentennial year.

On Saturday morning, December 20, at 5:20, the entire Wilson clan was up to watch Jim and Patty and Bob Hickey—who planned to run the first few miles—start their Las Vegas venture. Dotty had to work the first two days of the run, so she planned to join them later. Granddad Sturgis substituted for her until then.

Patty wore a blue T-shirt that covered her running shorts, and her long hair was tied at the nape of her neck. Jim's identifying trademark was his orange knit stocking cap. They were mismatched except for their black gloves, which seemed oddly, inappropriate to their scanty attire. It would be cold, but Patty hated the restriction of extra clothing and only wore the gloves in concession to Jim.

After their usual picture-taking session, Patty, Jim, and Bob sprinted out of Redwood Circle. They headed toward Orangethorpe Avenue, which led them across Orange County into the Santa Ana Canyon, onto a bicyclists path through Featherly Regional Park, and then to Sixth Street in Corona.

Patty had developed a runner's stride, but there were still traces of the old clumsiness. She'd never overcome her propensity for tripping and falling. In Placentia she twisted her ankle, but it was a minor injury. For the most part, that first thirty-mile day was uneventful, as was their second thirty-five mile day. Jim's favorite pastime, gleaning the roadway for coins and returnable bottles, yielded a meager four pennies and four bottles.

At 5:33 on the morning of the third day, Patty and Jim started up Cajon Pass to conquer their first mountain and their first freeway. They would be running over what had originally been part of the Old Spanish Trail. This trade-route to the California coast, which dated from the 1830s and began at Santa Fe, New Mexico, tracked north of the Grand Canyon into Paiute Indian country at Las Vegas Springs, a lush oasis in a death-trap desert. The Spanish Trail crossed into California through the Mojave Desert, eventually ascending Cajon Pass before concluding in Los Angeles.

On the sparsely inhabited stretches, where few cars passed, Jim and Patty began to sense the spirit of pioneers who had adventured across this unfamiliar land. They were beginning to comprehend things that modern travelers—encased in steel and glass, insulated from the excesses of cold and heat, cradled by upholstered seats—miss as they whip onward at freeway speeds.

Patty and Jim were learning a true sense of distance, in a way that can only be understood trekking by foot. They were discovering how wearying and difficult it is to cover the ground hour by hour, mile upon mile, day after day, and how high a mountain is when you have to run up it.

The sound of their steady footfalls trudging up Cajon Pass mingled with those of long-ago. Ghosts of Mexican muleteers with a score of horses and pack-laden mules seemed to clip-clop beside them, stirring the gray-brown earth with their hoofs and kicking up pebbles that bit the drivers' ankles. Patty and Jim printed their tire-tread shoe marks into the earth, but the rocks that grazed their legs were kicked up by tires of passing cars stirring the gravel on the sandy shoulder.

The Mexican muleteers and Patty and Jim shared common rou-

tines. Out at the touch of dawn, they were exposed to the extreme
cold, forfeiting breakfast and home. The horsemen had urged their
sleepy teams up the grade; Jim, full of fire, prodded Patty.

"Come on, Patty. Let's go! Get going! Come on! Quit dragging!"
After about an hour and a half, Jim chirped, "Good morning, Patty.
Glad you're awake."

Patty answered, "Where are we? How far have we gone?"

This was their morning ritual: Jim, Teddy Roosevelt charging San
Juan Hill, and Patty, running by pure instinct.

They stopped for brief rests at one mile, then five miles, and again
at the ten-mile mark. Patty suffered the indignity of no bathroom
facilities. Like the pioneer women, she had to abandon her pride,
dispense with her modesty (when the camper was nowhere near),
and relieve herself behind scraggy open-laced brush.

After eleven miles, the side road ended, and Patty and Jim started
their first freeway miles. Jim wore a brilliant orange T-shirt and Patty
wore a matching vest over her white shirt. They would be clearly
visible to passing motorists. Jim was afraid to run on the freeway, but
his fear turned to terror when they encountered an unexpected
phenomenon. Curious drivers, spotting them running along the
freeway shoulder, veered toward them, bringing tons of steel within
inches of the duo. Drivers of recreational vehicles, sitting to the left
in the driver's seat, forgot about their overhanging mirrors, which
could easily have injured Patty or Jim.

Beyond that danger, beyond the belching exhaust pipes and the
terrible stench of gas and oil fumes, Jim feared they'd be stopped by
the Highway Patrol. He had pinned the permission note to the front
of his pants, but he kept reminding Patty, "I know they're going to
stop us. We don't belong on the freeway."

His anticipation of what might happen intimidated Jim more than
the actual dangers they encountered. As they neared the top of the
grade, a Highway Patrol car pulled up beside them.

Jim retreated into his imagination and watched the scene as if he
were standing to one side. He saw Patty and himself standing there
in nylon shorts, T-shirts, and nothing else: they were exposed, almost completely naked. And the officer striding toward them resem-

bled John Wayne. He towered over them. He brushed aside his coat and tucked his hand on his gunbelt as if he were going to draw his gun at any moment and shoot them down.

Jim fumbled with the pin that held the permission note onto the front of his pants, trying to explain. The officer read the note, then waved them on with neither a smile nor a remark to soften the encounter.

Exhaustion, both physical and emotional, overwhelmed Jim. Just as the mules had strained to make the last few miles up the grade, their tongues lolling and chests heaving with each step, Patty and Jim strained too. They pushed and searched for every breath, craving oxygen, pulling each other along with an invisible psychological rein. They always ran at a conversational pace that enabled them to talk easily and keep each other psyched-up. Now their words were abbreviations, and it was the mere presence of the other that kept each running. Then they sighted the sign: "Cajon Summit. Elev. 4,190 Ft."

Euphoric, forgetting their pain, they flew the last hundred yards, slapping the signpost, a ritualistic gesture to identify their stopping spot. They'd touch it again when they started out, to symbolize Jim's meticulous sense of accuracy, his determination never to break their running thread.

They conquered their mountain in four hours and nine minutes. After Dotty took a picture of Jim and Patty next to the elevation sign, they drank some juice, rolled into their bunks, and slept. They could sleep almost any time in any place, and Dotty kept a bed made up for them in the camper.

After a twenty minute nap, Jim and Patty crested Cajon Pass. The highway stretched before them; the desert spread out below them. Nine miles to go! Dotty drove ahead to reserve a campsite and then returned to the thirty-mile spot where they planned to stop for that day.

The scale of life eventually balances itself. In the morning, Jim was fired with energy and Patty dragged. At the end of their day, Patty chattered, telling Jim stories about school, her teachers, her ups and downs, her thoughts and plans, while Jim was just hanging on. He couldn't say a thing; every muscle in his body strained and screamed, *Stop!*

Patty pulled her father. "Daddy, come on. You can make it if you don't quit."

White film edged Jim's mouth and he merely nodded his head toward Patty, running to her words. They played psychological games.

Jim rasped, "Go ahead, Patty! Leave me."

"No, I won't leave you," promised Patty.

"You can go ahead. I'll die, but you can leave me," wheezed Jim, in a joking tone.

"Mom will have a nice dinner for us."

"I'll never make it! I'll die hungry."

"It's just a little bit farther. See the camper?"

"Where?" Jim searched the road ahead of them.

"See it?" Patty pointed to a camper in the distance, parked beside the highway.

The camper, always their incentive, was the finish line. *None of the evils and dangers of the road are represented in that camper,* reflected Jim. *Everything good is there. Mother. Home. Bathroom. Food. Security. Safety.* He focused his thoughts. "Forget the fatigue and pain; just get to Mother."

As they raced toward the camper, Patty realized it wasn't theirs.

"It's not our camper!" Patty moaned.

They wanted to believe it was theirs, their minds had told them it was, but they had been deceived. Their drive, ballooned by anticipation, deflated. Depression sucked their energy away.

"Bite down on the bullet!" they said as one, then laughed together. It was the expression they used when they wanted to help each other overcome pain, discouragement, or anything that went wrong.

Dusk shadowed the desert floor. Jim and Patty were past exhaustion. Going up the mountain was a strain, but running down was worse because of the constant pounding and restraining to keep from racing. Knees are the shock absorbers of the body, and Patty's knees throbbed from absorbing the constant thump-thump, thump-thump of her feet pounding asphalt.

It was 4:50 when they finally slapped the rear of the camper parked at a drive-through hamburger stand near Victorville. With every step, they had donated their energy to the road; they crawled into the camper and crashed onto the bed. Richard, Sam, and Dotty sat in front as Richard drove to the campground.

Dotty had prepared supper, and Patty and Jim devoured their spaghetti like ravenous animals. They couldn't eat fast enough. After supper they took showers; then Dotty and Sam rubbed the runners' legs with a balm to loosen up the muscles and ligaments. By 5:45, Patty and Jim were lost in a deep sleep.

It was too cold for the rest of the family to be outside, yet too early to sleep. They couldn't listen to the radio or move around or they might disturb Jim and Patty. They spent their evening playing table games or cards, then turned in around eight, which was their usual nightly pattern.

The morning of the fourth day, Patty awoke in pain; her knees ached. At 5:40, the temperature was a hostile thirty-one degrees. Patty was not completely awake when they started out, and the pain had not fully reached her. They were only five miles from the hundred-mile mark. She tried to stifle her tears, but she couldn't. The streets were quiet, so quiet that Patty could hear herself crying.

"Come on, Patty," Jim encouraged.

"I hurt!" Patty's sobs echoed harder and louder with every step she ran.

"Try not to think about it."

Patty felt like she was crawling on the street. The pain ravaged her and she wept uncontrollably.

"Come on, Patty," urged Jim. "We can't stop! We have no way of contacting Mother. If we stop, we'll freeze to death. We have to keep moving."

Patty tried to divert her thoughts from the pain; she had trained herself to think about something else to keep herself running when she was extra hungry or fatigued. But the pain wouldn't allow her to concentrate on the two more miles they had to cover. *This is a terrible life! This pain will hurt me forever.*

"We'll decide whether to quit or go on when we reach the camper," Jim tried to console her, "but we have to get to Mother."

He urged her on, in his usual way, attempting to keep her moving.

Reaching the camper and the coveted hundred miles seemed a hollow success. Patty dragged herself into the camper and collapsed on the bed. Dotty had brought pain pills left over from a visit to the dentist. She gave one to Patty. After a brief rest, they sat around the table to determine whether they should go on.

"I don't want to make the decision now," Patty told her parents. "I don't feel good, but I don't feel bad. I just don't feel great."

Jim didn't know what to do. Did he have the right to let Patty go on? "How's the pain now?" he asked.

"Not too bad," Patty said tentatively.

"How bad?" questioned Dotty.

Patty massaged and pressed her knees to check the soreness, "They're not as bad as they were; I think the pain pills have helped."

"Maybe you should stop for the day," Dotty quietly suggested. Worry betrayed itself in her face.

"Patty says she feels better," Jim challenged, "Do you think you can run?"

"I think so, Daddy."

"Let's get going!"

They were now on the National Trails Highway near Oro Grande. In 1878, when gold was discovered in the Old Silver Mountain, the town boasted a population of two thousand. The range of mountains, chisled by mines and sandpapered by winds and flash floods, wore a rich rainbow coat of oranges, yellows, browns, and blacks. In the distance they appeared to be dressed in elegant shades of plums and purples. The tawny desert was desolate and harsh. To Jim, it was uttermost isolation; to Patty, it was pain. She limped through the next five miles.

After another pain pill and rest, Patty still wanted to run. The cross-country guys would rub it in if she quit. She had to work against that, she convinced herself. *I'll make it, pain or not. I will run three hundred miles!*

After their third five-mile set and another break, Richard drove Sam and Dotty to Victorville to buy elastic bandages for Patty's knees. Dotty planned to report Jim's and Patty's progress to their hometown papers, and do some shopping while Sam did the laundry.

The medication camouflaged Patty's pain, and she and Jim returned to their natural routine. They investigated a shell of a car, turned over like a turtle on its back. Further on they spotted an abandoned saloon and gas station. It was built of rocks, and painted a garish rose-pink. A white and red lettered sign invited: *Sage Brush Inn.* Two vintage gas pumps—one silver the other red—stood like sentinels, guarding the old building. The inn was boarded up.

"Come on!" Jim hissed. "Let's go around back and peek inside."

"Look, Daddy. One of the boards is missing."

Jim looked over his shoulder. No one was around. "C'mon, pardner. I'll give you a boost."

They crawled through the window and felt their way through the darkness. There were no lights and no illumination from the open window. Loose boards creaked under their feet.

"Oh!" Patty gasped. Jim could hear her falling, but he couldn't see her in the blackness. "Daddy! Help me!"

"Where are you?" Panic etched Jim's voice.

"I'm down here, Daddy. I fell through a hole in the floor!"

"Are you hurt?"

"No."

Jim searched the air and groped in front of him, fearing he'd fall. He lay on the floor next to the hole and reached down. His hand swept past Patty's in the darkness: then he touched her. He grabbed Patty's hands and pulled her out like a rag doll. They scrambled out of the window, grateful to be free and safe.

Afterwards, Jim was horrified. All the possibilities crowded in and accused him. Patty could have fallen into an endless hole. She could have broken her neck or legs or arms or back. There might have been snakes in the hole.

Jim knew the adage, "The desert is unforgiving to those who break its rules." The sandy plain with low grey brush possessed at once a hypnotic dullness and a strange serenity and stillness. A desolate land, it wove a web of unreality and lured Jim into its spell.

Jim had lost sense of time and distance. He had nothing to mark it by. He knew Dotty had been gone a long time, much longer than usual. Had they run ten miles or four since they'd left the Sage Brush Inn? Had it been a half hour or two?

At first, Jim played with the idea that Dotty had gone away and left them stranded. Then he labored with the thought that something had happened to her.

"Do you think the truck broke down?"

"How will Mom let us know?" asked Patty.

"She can't. There's no way she can communicate with us. Maybe she left us out here to die."

"Mom wouldn't leave us!"

"I don't think she would, but she's sure been gone too long. What if something happened to her? We'd better look for places where we could curl up and stay for the night. We'd die in the cold!"

"Where? There's nothing!" Patty swept her hand toward the empty, brush-studded landscape.

"There's nothing to protect us!" Jim's fears turned into panic. "You can see how people must feel when they've been stranded by an airplane crash, or their car breaks down or something. They wander aimlessly. Everything looks the same. Can't you imagine how people become delirious and hungry and thirsty in the heat?"

"I *am* thirsty!" Patty's tongue felt like dry, dead wood.

"There's no water, not a drop of water anywhere."

Ordinarily, Patty didn't worry. It wasn't her nature. Her faith in her father was a simple child's trust. It wasn't something she thought about openly, it was something she felt and intensely believed. She was safe with Daddy. He'd rescue her. He'd keep her from danger.

But now that he had drawn her into his fears, she cried. She was afraid. This wasn't a part of their silly banter. The piercing cold cut through her sweatshirt and nylon shorts and intensified the pain in her knees.

"There's no phone. No human beings," Jim rambled on. "Only rattlesnakes. Pretty soon the buzzards will start circling us."

When Dotty caught up to them, Jim shouted, "Why were you gone so long? You left us to die. We really thought we were going to *die!*" Jim flared into a tirade. "Look! Do you see? There's nothing out here to protect us. Nothing to save us! Nothing! We were freezing. We were dying of thirst. We could have died!"

Dotty had been away only an hour and a half, while Jim and Patty ran ten miles. Dotty, the soother, calmed Jim, but the stress tore at her. Her continual fears for her family's safety eroded her strength. The tensions, fears, and fatigue stripped them all, made them raw, and drove them to emotional extremes.

Jim was as remorseful as he had been frightened and angry: he knew the trip was hard on Dotty. He worried about her. What was it doing to her? She drank gallons of coffee worrying about them. She bit her nails. She was distraught. The one thing he hated was the detrimental effect the trip was having on her.

To make it up, Jim apologized, then tried to lessen Dotty's tension with humor. Laughter tranquilized them both, at least momentarily, but by the end of the afternoon they were so extremely exhausted that they wondered if their minds could rest sufficiently to carry them through another day.

Christmas Eve morning Jim and Patty were outside Barstow. The constantly shifting weather was sometimes their ally, sometimes their enemy. Nippy winds taunted them, then skipped away, only to jump out at them again. The air steadily warmed from the high twenties to the low fifties as the morning wore on.

During their breaks, Jim assessed the temperature and looked at the sky to see what mood it was in. If Patty and he wore too much clothing, it became a burdensome pack in the heat; if they wore too little, they risked chilling themselves. Today, Jim was thankful; the sky was watercolor blue, cloudless, with no sign of rain—or worse —the snow he continually expected.

Mid-morning, they were to run on another section of freeway. Dotty wanted to take a picture of them beside a new sign on the side of their camper. It advertised: "Running 300 miles La Palma to Las Vegas, Patty & Jim Wilson." The owner of the Calico campground had lettered the sign for them because she felt they needed to announce their run.

Patty and Jim were standing by a gas station, clowning around.

When they turned to smile for Dotty, they saw to their horror that she was sprawled on the ground. When she had turned to get a better picture, she had bumped right into a metal frame that had once held panels posting gasoline prices. She was semi-conscious and bleeding profusely from a laceration on her forehead.

"Bring me a towel, Sam!" Jim yelled.

"May I help?" the gas station attendant asked as he bent down beside Jim. Richard and Patty were staring at Dotty.

"Call an ambulance!"

"Oh, no! I can't go to the hospital!" objected Dotty.

"Honey, I can't stop the bleeding." Jim and Sam had been frantically trying to stanch the spurting stream of blood.

When the paramedics arrived, they whisked Dotty onto a stretcher and into the sterile cocoon of the ambulance.

I can't stay in the hospital, Dotty agonized. *Jim and Patty shouldn't run on the freeway without me. It's unsafe for them to be alone. What if I've ruined the trip for them? No! I can't! They have to run thirty miles today. It will mean extra days if they don't. Maybe I could get another day off work? No, I can't do that.* Dotty negotiated her options, then settled on a plan. *I'll tell Jim and Patty to go on without me. Richard can drive. Sam can cook; she can take care of them.*

Soon after Dotty was wheeled into the emergency room at Barstow Community Hospital, she instructed the nurse, "Please tell my husband and daughter I'm okay and to go ahead. Tell them Richard can come back to check on me."

Richard drove Patty and Jim to the freeway while Dotty had her head stitched. She was thankful her hair didn't have to be shaved; the cut was at the hairline. Richard signed his mother out of the hospital. She was relieved that her injury hadn't interfered with the run; Patty and Jim put in a thirty-mile day. Christmas Eve they crossed the halfway mark: 157 miles.

Thursday, December 25, Patty moved through her usual morning ritual. Bathroom first. Get dressed. Do warm-up exercises. Push away from the wall. Bend down, grab the back of the heels, and bring head to ankles. Wrap knees in elastic bandages. Drink a glass of juice. Glance at the time. 5:30! Brace for the cold. Remember? It's Christmas.

"Today's Christmas, Daddy!"

"I thought you forgot. Merry Christmas, Patty."

Neither Jim's nor Patty's spirits were psyched for running, they were only covering three-mile intervals. On a section of freeway between Field and Dunn roads, a Highway Patrol car pulled them over. While the mustached patrolman approached, Jim again struggled to unpin the permission note.

"Don't bother with that. You're okay," the patrolman gestured. "You're clear all the way to Nevada. I just wanted to meet the nut who would make his daughter run on the freeway Christmas day." He turned to Patty. "Wouldn't you rather be home around a Christmas tree stacked with presents and have a nice turkey dinner cooking in the oven?"

The patrolman was superb in his attempt to make Jim feel absolutely miserable, but Patty responded without hesitation, "No! I'd rather be out here with my Dad."

The officer smiled incredulously. "Have a Merry Christmas."

"Thanks for the vote of confidence," Jim told Patty as the patrolman drove away. "That was super!"

Jim and Patty finished their thirty-mile day at 3:05; now the family could have their celebration. They located a trailer park in the town of Baker. Jim hadn't shaved, and he was grubby and sweaty when he knocked at the manager's door. As the door opened, the fragrance of Christmas embraced him; there were scattered wrappings and presents, a trimmed tree, and a table laden with a feast. The family inside appeared to be in a joyful, festive mood.

The manager paused to read the sign on the side of the Wilson's camper. Then she smiled and said, "You can have any site you choose. It's our Christmas present!"

"Thanks!" beamed Jim.

After Patty and he had taken showers, the family planned to open one gift each and have dinner. At home, Dotty had baked a turkey, sliced it, carefully wrapped it in foil, and put it in the ice box. But when Jim and Patty returned to the camper, Dotty was sobbing.

"What's the matter?" Jim asked, horrified.

"The turkey!" The words came from her tear-choked throat. "The turkey's gone!"

"We took everything out of the ice box, but we couldn't find it," offered Sam.

"It didn't walk out," Jim contended. "It's got to be in here somewhere."

"It's gone! Sam, Richard, and I looked everywhere. It isn't here," Dotty wept.

"Maybe it fell into the trash. It's right under the ice box," suggested Jim.

"Yeah, Richard. Did you throw the turkey away?" Patty accused.

"I never saw it!" Richard's eyes widened. "It wasn't me!"

"It didn't fly away!" snapped Jim.

"Well, I didn't throw it out!" Richard protested.

"Maybe Dad accidentally took the turkey when he went home," defended Dotty.

"So, Granddad stole the turkey," laughed Jim.

Later, when they called Grandma and Granddad Sturgis to wish them a Merry Christmas, Granddad reported he hadn't even seen the package of turkey and had no idea what could have happened. They could only surmise that it might have gone out with the trash. Their lost-turkey teasing settled into depression, subduing them during their dinner of leftovers and macaroni and cheese.

"Dad, I'll do anything you suggest, anything you plan." Patty broke the solemn spirit with her plea. "But next time—please! Let's not be gone for Christmas! It's too lonely."

"I miss the whole family being together," Sam put in.

"I know," answered Jim. "My Mom, and Nana, and Grandma and Granddad probably don't know what to do without us. They're alone. They've always had Christmas at our house, and suddenly we aren't there."

"The tree I bought for home was only up two days," Richard said wistfully.

"I used to groan about how much work it was to have everybody at our house," Dotty murmured, "but it's worth it! This experience will always make me appreciate Christmas!"

"I know," Jim slumped down. "We lost Christmas, didn't we?"

8 Running Down the Yellow Brick Road

DECEMBER 26, the seventh day. Baker, California, once a bustling mining town, sleeps lazily between Soda Mountain and Soda Dry Lake. In the 1860s, history—the western movie kind—was enacted there. The US Army camped on the hard-baked lakebed and sent small companies of soldiers into the desert in search of Indians who had been ambushing travelers.

Like those adventurers sitting around the campfires swapping stories, Patty and Jim carried on a continuous western saga in a silly sort of way.

"Cum on, Tressie True-Heart. Cain't ya run faster?" drawled Jim.

"I'z runnin' as fast as I kin, Hillbilly," Patty twanged.

"Look at them thar fellars over yonder." Like grizzled miners, several elderly men, their features chiseled by the harsh desert weather, rocked on the porch of a ramshackle house.

"They shore is gawking at us funny-like, Hillbilly."

"You gat your shoe untied, Tressie True-Heart?"

"You got yor britches undone?"

"Nope."

"Think they'll ketch us, Hillbilly?"

"Not a chance. Hey, look at them thar bottles."

"But, Hillbilly! We cain't carry no more. Look at ya now."

Hillbilly snickered; he clenched three bottles in one hand and four in the other. Tressie True-Heart was carrying four, plus a license plate.

"Them thar is gold, Tressie. We'll bring Ma back to get 'em."

Bottles. Multicolored schools of every species and size swam for mile upon mile in this vast desert-sea. Dotty now waited for Jim and Patty at the end of every set with a bucket for all their bottles.

Dotty said to Sam, "Here comes your father with his ever-loving bottles."

"I found a gold mine of bottles," exclaimed Jim.

"Oh Jim! You've got to be kidding! We've got bottles coming out of our ears. We've stuffed them everywhere in this camper. They're moving us out. We'll have to sleep with them."

"You can cash them in at the market."

"They refuse to take them; they don't want to bother with them."

Richard drove them back to Jim's bottle mine and they found twenty-seven returnable bottles. "Don't you let any break," Jim warned. "Not one!"

Patty set one on the cab and it rolled off and shattered on the pavement.

"I told you guys to be careful!" shouted Jim. "I don't want one more bottle broken!"

Dotty rolled her eyes.

"Ahhh, come on, Dad," growled Richard.

"Sam, get that license plate over there," pointed Jim.

"But, Jim!" sputtered Dotty. "We have so many California and Nevada plates, the police will think we're running a hot car ring if they stop us."

"They're souvenirs of our trip!"

Crawling at a turtle's pace twenty-five to thirty miles a day over the same straight ribbon highway bored Richard and Sam, who had almost nothing to do. They entertained themselves by lining up bottles like traitors before a firing squad, or setting up penny arcade games and pelting the bottles with rocks.

"I've never broken so many bottles or been so bored in my entire life," Richard confided to his mother. "I don't ever want to go on another trip. I'll stay home and work the next time!"

When Patty and Jim stopped that day, they had netted one penny and fifty-seven bottles from the desert floor.

Saturday, December 27, Patty and Jim were near Holloran Springs. Their silly saga was no longer Hillbilly and Tressie True-Heart, instead, their fantasy had become Dorothy's adventures from the Wizard of Oz. They pretended that Las Vegas was the Emerald City. The seemingly endless Baker grade over their second mountain was like following the yellow brick road. Patty was Dorothy; her father was not only the great Oz, but all of her companions.

"When Dorothy stood in the doorway and looked around, she could see nothing but the great gray prairie on every side."* From horizon to horizon, Patty could see nothing but the barren desert. Gray hung quietly above the beige earth, the low smoke colored brush, and the silent, contorted Joshua trees. Even the silence seemed gray.

When the cyclone struck, Dorothy was picked up from her home on the Kansas prairies, only to wake up in the strange land of Oz. Patty felt as if that had happened to her. Her only wish, like Dorothy's, was to get back home. To her, La Palma was a beautiful place, where even the winter grass was green. There were water fountains, and roses in bloom, and ripe-polished oranges hung from the trees.

To dispel the gloom, Patty loved to sing when they ran. She belted out popular songs, and some of Dorothy's, like "Over the rainbow." But Patty wondered if her father's magic would ever get her home again, where she could be in her own room and sleep in her own bed? Running the long silent stretches and being away from familiar surroundings robbed Patty of something she couldn't define. Their family was together, yet her father and she were alone. She despaired of ever seeing her friends again; she had been away too long, and she missed them.

"Patty! Patty! *Patty!*" A voice echoed through her daydreams.

She looked up in time to catch a glimpse of one of her classmates. The upper half of her body was hanging out the car window as her parents were speeding down the freeway, and she was waving and screaming.

*L. Frank Baum, *The Wizard of Oz* (San Raphael, Cal.: Classic Publishing Corporation, 1970), p. 9.

"Patty! Patty! *Patty!*"

"Daddy! That was one of the girls from school. She told me she'd look for me," exclaimed Patty.

Now Patty ran briskly toward her Emerald City. Her shoes, like Dorothy's, thumped merrily down the gray ribbon highway. There were no bluebirds to serenade her, no flowers or rainbows to cheer her, no sun to embrace her. But she didn't feel nearly as depressed as she had, despite being "whisked away from her own country and set down in the midst of a strange land" (p. 24).

After Patty and Jim had crested the Baker grade and were loping down the backside of the mountain, past Mountain Pass, they saw a rest area. Just as Patty was darting toward the bathroom, a lady saw her.

"Oh!" the woman exclaimed. "You're the little girl who's running to Las Vegas, aren't you?"

Patty nodded and smiled.

"We read about you in the *Register,*" the woman continued. "Could you do us a favor? My friends here," she gestured toward an elderly couple sitting in a car, "are deaf mutes. They were so hopeful that we might see you running along the road. Now here you are in person! Would it be possible for them to have a picture taken with you? I know they would treasure it dearly."

While Patty and Jim were having their picture taken with the couple, Patty gritted her teeth and whispered, "I've got to go to the bathroom so bad. If only they knew."

"Shhh!" Jim admonished, and smiled.

"They can't hear me!" Patty hissed back.

When Patty woke the morning of the ninth day, it was bitterly cold. The running was not all that good; their blisters had developed blisters, and they were popping and oozing blood. They had run 245 miles.

Patty continued to ask, "How much farther is it to Las Vegas?"

"I don't know. It seems like forever," lamented Jim.

After running thirteen and a half miles, Patty and Jim arrived at the state line. Dotty snapped a picture of Patty and Jim posing by a "Welcome to Nevada" sign. Patty thought Border Town was a sleazy place, and they were all surprised to see slot machines.

The blisters on Jim and Patty's feet and toes burst and stung and burned. They each knew the other was hurting, but rather than complain, they clenched their jaws and continued to run.

Now Jim was the Tin Woodman, who had wept "tears of sorrow and regret" because he accidently killed a small creature, "for he was always careful not to hurt any living thing" (p. 49). Jim grieved when he looked at Patty. He kept asking himself, *Why am I doing this to one that I love? What is the point? Why do I torture her?*

They were both tired. Super tired! Their muscles screamed for rest. Jim gathered up what little strength he had to give to Patty, and she gave it back to him.

Jim was so proud of Patty he could not contain it. She was not only Dorothy; she had been like the timid lion, who thought he lacked courage but was in truth very courageous. Jim admired her fearlessness, her will to keep running, her refusal to give up, her growing confidence, and—most of all—her courage.

Theirs was a unique bond, an unplanned closeness. Jim wished everyone could experience it. Traveling the road together, escaping dangers, sharing hardships, living out this Wizard of Oz adventure, their spirits soared joyously high.

> The next morning, as soon as the sun was up, they started on their way, and soon saw a beautiful green glow in the sky just before them.
> "That must be the Emerald City," said Dorothy.
> The green glow became brighter and brighter, and it seemed that at last they were nearing the end of their travels" (p. 77).

There was Las Vegas! Finally it was in front of them glistening in the distance. The hotels and other buildings of the gray-green city rose out of the sagebrush plain, then disappeared when Patty and Jim dipped down into a shallow valley, only to reappear when they ran to the top of a knoll.

Patty and Jim were skipping and hopping down the yellow brick road singing with gusto, "We're off to see the Wizard." Patty broke out laughing. Jim bowed. They danced on, breaking into giggles as they tried to finish the song.

Then, they raced faster and faster. After they had run and run and run, animated by an intense and joyful energy and vigor, they suddenly realized the glow from the Emerald City was much farther away then they had thought. They had to slow to a disappointing pace.

When they finally neared Las Vegas, they could see the Silver Slipper Hotel. They were running down The Strip, the traffic was bumper to bumper, and the people were shoulder to shoulder. Their mood was festive because it was New Year's weekend.

The hilarious spirit of the people heightened Patty's excitement. She and Jim were both relieved and joyous to be nearing the end. This was ecstasy! They'd finally made it! Yet Jim regretted that his great fantasy, this magnificent adventure, would soon be over and he would have to return to the mundane working life.

Patty was disappointed when they had to give up at 288.2 miles, near the Star Dust Hotel. They just couldn't push their way through the celebrating crowd.

The morning of December 30, they were out at nine o'clock. Jim figured the celebrators would be sleeping in; perhaps they could complete their run unhampered. Patty and he were on the corner of Las Vegas Boulevard and Freemont Street, pushing the "walk" button, when a lady pulled up in front of them. Recognition lit her face.

"Oh, aren't you that little girl that lives in Orange County?" she pointed through the window.

Patty waved to the lady, who had to drive on.

"Can you believe that, Patty? Someone recognized you this far away from home!" exclaimed Jim. "You've become a real celebrity! One day your name could be up on one of those billboards in bright lights!"

Patty looked up at her father and smiled shyly. It did give her a warm feeling to be recognized, but she wasn't too sure she wanted to be in the bright lights.

Jim and Patty finished their final 11.8 miles on Freemont Street and Missouri Avenue at 11:40, an anticlimax compared to the previous day. They had collected thirty-one cents and stuffed 187 returnable bottles into every nook and corner of their camper.

To celebrate, the Wilsons went to a smorgasbord at the Hacienda Hotel that evening. There were all types of food and desserts to choose from.

"You've earned yourself a treat," Jim told Patty. "You've deprived yourself. You've pushed yourself, and you've run three hundred miles! Now, let yourself go. You can have anything to eat or any amount. If you want enchiladas and roast beef, or twenty pieces of pie and a hundred scoops of ice cream, eat it. Eat anything you want!"

Patty ate everything she desired, but since she hadn't been eating rich foods, it was too much for her. After dinner, the Wilsons went to the MGM Grand Hotel and strolled through the lobby. Patty's stomach revolted at the concoctions she had eaten, and before she had time to escape, she lost her dinner all over the lush carpeting of the lobby. She was whitish-green. She couldn't stop herself from vomiting, yet all she could think of was that she was throwing up on the expensive carpet of the multi-million-dollar hotel.

"I'm sorry. I'm sorry," she cried, fearing that the hotel would charge her parents for cleaning or replacing the carpet. She kept apologizing to her father. "Oh, Daddy, I'm sorry. You bought me a nice dinner. I loved it so much! It cost you so much money and now I've wasted it."

"Patty, don't worry about it. The carpet will be fine." Jim tried to console her. "I should have known you couldn't handle a rich meal like that after running so much."

The next day, after Patty recovered, Jim and she talked to the local news reporters and told them of their successful adventure.

Dorothy's shoes had wonderful powers. They could take her wherever she wished to go in only three steps, and each step was made in the wink of an eye. All she had to do was knock the heels together and command the magic shoes to carry her to Kansas. She had found the truth: "There's No Place Like Home." And Patty's heart's desire, now, was that Granddad's camper would carry her home.

But Jim was thinking about Patty's shoes and their magnificent posibilities. Driving home New Year's Day, he turned to Patty and asked, "Well, Patty, are you ready to run to San Francisco in June?"

9 *San Francisco Sunstroke*

FOR PATTY, January first to June tenth whisked by in the wink of an eye and three taps of her silver shoes. During that interlude Jim and Patty worked up to eighty, then to one hundred miles a week in their San Francisco training sessions, with a brief pause for girls' track.

Patty had a rigorous, grueling routine. Every day after school, she had the regular warm-up exercises and speed intervals—110s, 220s, 440s, 880s, 1310s—for her school track team. Every morning or evening, and sometimes both, she ran ten to fifteen miles, plus twenty miles a day on weekends, building up endurance for San Francisco.

Patty won seven out of nine dual meets in that time, but just before league finals, she pulled a muscle in her right foot. She taped her foot, but it was so swollen she could barely squeeze it into her shoe. Despite the discomfort, she qualified for third and was able to compete in the one mile. But her time was slow and she was out in lane seven.

Patty's first three steps were her fastest. She tried to ignore the pain, but she couldn't. Her foot slapped and dragged the ground. She knew the people on the sidelines could see she was hurting.

She dropped behind to last place when an automatic timer turned on the lawn sprinklers, soaking her and puddling the dirt in front of her. She hobbled across the finish line. Although she felt it was her worst race, she was proud that she hadn't quit. Her teammates were proud of her, too, and she was voted most inspirational runner for that season.

To Jim, engineering the San Francisco trip was almost harder than running it would be. He tried for clearance on the freeway and was given an unequivocal *no.* Instead, he chose a bike trail paralleling the aqueduct system that threads its way through central California.

He wrote to television stations and government officials to solicit an audience for Patty's send-off and arrival. He called papers in Orange County, Los Angeles, and San Francisco to see if they would print the story of the proposed trip, and asked local papers to invite the public and runners to come see them off.

June 11, 1976. "San Francisco or Bust," the paper banner proclaimed. Patty shot through it as if propelled by a slingshot. Her mane of blonde hair billowed behind her.

"Hey, Patty, we're not running the hundred yard dash!" one of the runners yelled.

Over one hundred neighbors, friends, reporters, photographers, and members of the Junior Women's Club applauded as the host of runners disappeared around the corner of Redwood Circle. They milled around in the middle of the street and finished cups of coffee and donuts.

"Five o'clock in the morning!" someone growled.

Dotty thanked the well-wishers, then joined her parents in loading the camper. It was decorated with a huge red and black sign announcing, "Patty Wilson running 500 miles from La Palma to San Francisco to break her world record. CHEER HER ON."

Pete Strudwick and county supervisor Laurence Schmit accompanied them for the first few miles, but Patty and Jim concluded their first forty-mile day alone on San Fernando Road. June 12, the daylight lingered. The sun rose at 5:40 and would set at 8:06, leaving the full moon to stand in its space. The tidal pull of the full moon, is often accused of affecting our moods. Perhaps it was this mysterious power that possessed the afternoon.

At high noon, Patty and Jim were running in slow motion, their energy evaporated by the especially energetic sun. Jim kept looking back to check on Patty, who lagged a half-block behind. A few minutes later, he glimpsed a man standing on the grassy parkway twenty feet or so ahead.

The man was cutting and stabbing at the air with a long butcher knife. In a matter of seconds, Jim was past him. The man's face was contorted by a demented grin. Surely he saw Jim, but Jim could not discern any sign of recognition in the young man's dark, dilated eyes.

Jim stopped and turned, facing the sidewalk where Patty would pass the man, who now had the knife raised as if to spring and stab. It was happening so quickly! Jim frantically tried to compute his options.

Should he yell at Patty? No, he might startle the man. She'd stop in the middle of the sidewalk. Was the man joking? Was he serious? Jim unconsciously reached to his waist as if to draw out a weapon. His imagination frightened him with images of Patty stabbed and dying.

Come on Patty! Hurry up! He gestured violently, making soundless contortions with his mouth, urging her to speed up.

But the entire scene—and Patty—plodded before Jim in slow motion. She neared the man with the butcher knife, oblivious of both him and Jim. The man didn't move. Did he see her? He slashed the air. Jim's muscles twitched like those of a race horse straining at the starting gate. Patty was within six feet of the knife's tip when she trudged by him. They still didn't seem to see each other.

"Come on! Pick it up!" Jim tried to subdue his hysteria. *"Let's move it!"*

"What's wrong?" she called.

"I'll tell you as we go. Let's just get out of here!"

Jim's well-oiled, rhythmic movements propelled him across the asphalt. Patty's stride was short, her feet pumping, her high kick barely missing her bottom. She strained and pressed to keep her father's pace. After three blocks Jim slowed to their usual lope and glanced back to see if the man were anywhere behind them. He wasn't.

"Did you see the man with the butcher knife?" Jim burst out, gasping for breath.

"No! I didn't see him!"

"He was within a foot of you."

"What was he doing?"

"He was raising a knife as if to stab you!" Jim spoke dramatically, demonstrating the man's stance.

"He was!" Patty's eyes widened, flashing horror.

"There's Mother!" Jim pointed.

Relief spread through Jim and Patty; they felt that odd mixture of fear and euphoria that follows a terrifying encounter. To see the camper and Mother waiting for them heightened their desire for safety and comfort. Jim felt as if they were returning home for the first time after a year in a terrible war.

The sun turned its oven up to a hundred degrees. California was in a drought, and the atmosphere was hot and as dry and brittle as brown paper.

Their third and fourth thirty-mile days, Patty and Jim passed through the desert communities of Lancaster, Rosamond, and Mojave. Six months earlier they had been in another part of this vast desert. Then it was cold and hostile and hypnotic. Now the sun fired the sandy earth in its kiln and made it burn.

Jim had tried to imagine what it would be like to be stranded in the desert in this kind of extreme heat, but the reality was worse than his fears. The desert stretched before them as infinite and arid as the slick, sun-bleached sky.

They started at a quarter to five so they could complete the majority of their miles during the coolest hours. They covered five miles each of the first two sets, then limited themselves to three, then to one mile or less as the hot day wore on. They guzzled gallons of water and juices and—although some runners consider the practice dangerous—they chewed salt tablets. They finished exhausted at 6:40 the fourth day.

The morning of June 15 they were out at 4:50. The temperature soared to 105 degrees, and delinquent winds incited a rash of fires throughout the state. Patty and Jim were grateful to be out of the heavy smog of the Los Angeles basin, and in a ranching area— although the only evidence they saw of the ranch homes were rows of rural mailboxes along the highway.

At mid-morning Dotty was putting in her daily mile. Jim, Patty, and she were running through a field when a man on horseback galloped up to them, shouting, "Run for the fence!"

They turned to see a herd of cattle charging at them! Cowboys, urging their horses to the front of the thundering herd, waved their hats and whooped, "Hi! Yi!" in an attempt to turn the cattle before they trampled the Wilsons. Dust rose from their hooves, smoking the air. The trio sprinted and scrambled like rodeo clowns escaping a bucking bull. They reached a barbed-wire fence, but there was no time to crawl under it.

The cattle turned in front of the Wilsons like a parade of rumbling army tanks. They were safe! But what they saw further down the road almost convinced them the torrid weather was causing hallucinations. At first they didn't want to admit aloud to each other what they thought they saw grazing with the cows.

"We're not seeing what we think we're seeing," Jim said.

"I didn't see it. Did you?" Dotty turned to Patty.

"Not me!"

"If we all say we didn't see it, why is it out there sneering at us?" Jim asked in a mock serious tone. "We're not on the Sahara Desert, it only feels like it!"

"It's the heat! You're hallucinating," snickered Dotty.

"It is a camel! A one-humped camel. We'd all agree to that, wouldn't we?"

"Nope! I never saw it!" Dotty shook her head.

"Me either!" laughed Patty.

They were later told that animals from an exotic farm had been sold to people in that area. The rancher had bought a camel and put it out with his cows.

That afternoon, in the Tehachapi area, they found they'd routed themselves to a dead end. There didn't seem to be a road over the mountain to Arvin. If they didn't locate at least a path, they'd lose their entire day's mileage. They would have to take a lengthy detour, and that meant extra days which they could not afford. The Wilsons stopped to ask local residents if there were a road over the mountain and were told there wasn't one. The people knew prospectors had crossed over the mountain in the late 1800s, but now there was nothing, not even a path. Finally, a lady rancher told them, "I think there's a sheep trail, but I'm not sure if it goes all the way."

After they located the head of the trail, they put in their remaining day's mileage. They had passed through the desert into an oasis of ranches, and now the trail led them into the wilderness. The land had been seared by the heat and was stripped of all but straw-like vegetation.

The next morning brought them near Horsethief Flats. Granddad Sturgis had decided to attempt the trail with the camper, even though it didn't have four-wheel drive. The trail meandered down ravines, through gulleys, and over the softly contoured hills. It was a single lane wide, and should another vehicle meet them head-on, there would be no space to turn out. The truck swaggered and bounced along with light dust puffing up behind it like Indian smoke signals. The camper inched by staggering drop-offs, setting off avalanches of dirt at the rim. Logs, chuck holes, and boulders had to be skirted carefully.

At first the only signs of life, other than Patty's and Jim's trudging steps, were jackrabbits and an occasional bird coasting and circling above them. Suddenly, Jim spotted a snake camoflouged against the dry, bare ground.

"There's a rattlesnake!" he exclaimed.

"Where?" asked Dotty, who was running with him.

"Right there by that rock," he pointed.

Dotty bent down. "I don't see it!" She started to crouch closer.

"Don't move!" cautioned Jim.

The rattler raised its head and made a quiet whirring sound.

Dotty screamed and backed away. "I didn't see it! It was so close!"

Now Jim became skittish. Every branch or twig resembled a snake. By noon it was 106 degrees. The dusty, hot air wilted Patty and Jim and stole their energy. For every two or three miles they ran, they took a two or three hour break.

When Patty and Jim crested the crown of the last ridge, the trail fell sharply. Furrowed farm lands covered the flatland below them like multi-hued corduroy quilts, and the sight filled them with exhileration. When they swooped down the steep path, they felt as if they were parachuting into Arvin.

Talking with the townspeople along their route was Jim's favorite pastime. He loved to astonish and thrill them with his adventures. Patty stood shyly watching her father, drawing pleasure from the funny way he entertained people.

"Where did you come from?" one Arvin resident asked.

"We came across the Tehachapi mountains." Jim's eyes danced, knowing he'd provoke a reaction.

"But there's no way you could come across the mountains!" exclaimed the resident.

"Well, we did!"

"There's no road. There's no path! There's nothing!"

"I know, but we came over the sheep trail."

"The sheep trail! That's impossible! No one even hikes up there."

"The truck made it over the rocks, over the logs, and through the gulleys. We made it and we're here!" grinned Jim.

The people just stood there, amazed, shaking their heads. At a service station, Jim told their story to a minister who was fretting over his spewing radiator and dented fender. The minister immediately forgot the accident he'd just been in and insisted on getting the local news reporter. This was a story for the paper! The reporter turned out to be the minister's wife. Jim was thrilled that they'd have some publicity, even in this little town in the middle of nowhere.

It was seven-thirty in the evening before they clocked in thirty miles at Pumpkin Center. The summer sun settled down late, and the coolness of evening never came.

Patty, Jim, Dotty, and Granddad hardly slept. There was no air-conditioning in the camper and the blanket of air they were under was far too warm. When dawn came, the sun cast its furious flame upon the earth.

Camper living was close living, and with the intense heat, tensions escalated. Jim and Granddad were arguing. He insisted that Jim and

Patty should be wearing hats to protect themselves from the sun, and kept urging them to put in forty miles a day.

Jim stubbornly insisted, "I don't have Patty do anything that I won't do. It's awful easy for someone to say, 'Go chop down those trees,' or 'Go mow the lawn and why aren't you working faster,' if you're the one who's giving the orders. If you were out there doing it yourself, you'd understand. I'm dying from the heat and Patty is too!"

"Then you should wear a hat and so should Patty," insisted Granddad stubbornly.

"Patty can't stand to wear too much clothing. She hates to wear a hat. I'm not going to wear one either!" shouted Jim.

By eleven o'clock it was 105 degrees and the camper thermometer peaked at 120 degrees in the direct sunlight. They had run fifteen miles and were at the beginning of the California aqueduct system. It was a cool and welcome relief to see the water. But the hope that the fresh blue water would cool them was just an illusion. There were no trees and no shade on this portion of the waterway. The concrete and sandy dirt retained the heat, which was especially distressing to Jim, who was becoming nauseated.

"Honey, I've got to stop. I'm sick!"

"You're putting me on," she replied.

"Really, I'm dying. I can't go on."

"Are you kidding me?"

"I have a horrible headache. I feel weak."

"Come on, Daddy. You'll be all right."

"Patty, I'm serious! I'm so sick I feel like quitting and going home. I can't stand this heat."

"Oh, you won't quit! I know you won't!"

Jim's image of invincibility had backfired. *It's really kind of funny,* he thought. *No matter what I say to her, I don't think she'll really believe how desperately sick I am and that I really want to quit.*

The nausea in his stomach expanded and rushed through his body. His limbs ached. He felt slightly uncoordinated and delirious. His head floated away from him, the bright water burned his eyes, and the ground danced and swirled before him.

"Are you all right, Daddy?" Patty suddenly realized that her father wasn't teasing.

"I think I've taken too many salt tablets." His mouth suddenly turned dry, too dry to swallow, too dry to talk. Jim forced one foot in front of the other until he reached the camper.

Granddad drove them to a nearby campground to rest under some shade trees. Dotty bathed Jim with water, trying to cool him. His nausea started to ease and he ate some lunch, thinking that it would make him feel better. Patty stretched out on a blanket to take a nap, and Dotty hand-washed some laundry and strung it all over the picnic tables.

Jim and she were resting on a bench when the nausea surged through Jim again. He retched, then vomited violently. Just when he thought it would pass, the nausea came in great rushing waves and he vomited again and again.

Sickness was something Jim refused to tolerate or accept in himself. There were no excuses, and he would not give in to it. Against Dotty's objections, he decided Patty and he would run another section of the aqueduct. It was 12:30 and the afternoon heat was blistering. Vehicles were not allowed on the path along the canal, which meant Granddad would drive the truck ahead and wait for them at a crossing road.

Jim knew he shouldn't have tried to continue. He was somewhat delirious by the time he reached the crossing at the four-and-a-half-mile mark. It was 1:15 and they'd completed twenty miles that day.

Jim slept all afternoon, but he felt wretched when he woke. An edge of nausea and headache stayed with him. Dotty was convinced he'd had a sunstroke and she begged him to give up and go home.

They had a family council and Patty quietly watched her father and mother and Granddad bickering. She remembered the council they'd had over her during the Las Vegas trip when her knees were so bad. They had been so serious when they talked about her quitting. "She's still so young. The rest of her life she'll limp," they had said.

Now she listened to her father persuading her mother and Granddad to go on, convincing them that he'd just taken too many salt pills. *He brushes off pain so lightly,* Patty thought. *Daddy doesn't baby himself as much as I do. He won't listen to pain. I try not to, but I still do.*

Friday morning, the eighth day, they were at the Buttonwillow fishing access. They started at 3:50, hoping to avoid the intensity of the heat, but Jim had to keep antacid tablets with him at all times. If he waited too long to take them, he couldn't drink water or juices and the urge to vomit returned. Incredibly, Jim and Patty still ran twenty-two miles that day, before driving to Bakersfield to pick Sam up at the bus station.

Saturday, the ninth day, they were out at 4:40 and completed nineteen miles by ten o'clock. It was 107 degrees and the sun raged upon Kettleman Hills when they started their last segment at 11:15. They would have to run fourteen miles, because there were no crossroads any sooner. Dotty, Granddad, and Sam drove ahead, then Sam rode her bicycle back to Patty and Jim at the seven-mile mark. She brought them a canteen of water and a radio. She would ride with them to keep them company. They were thankful to have her with them and grateful to have water. They drank long, satisfying gulps from the canteen and the liquid soothed their throats and mouths. Jim devoured antacid tablets to settle his stomach.

They climbed down the ladders along the waterway and soaked their shirts and headbands. They yearned to dip themselves in the water, so innocent and inviting; but workers along the canal had repeatedly warned them that there had been numerous drownings, including police and fire personnel attempting rescues. The current was swift, and slippery green moss grew on the funnelshaped sides. Jim was convinced of the danger after he dangled his shirt too near a pump. It chewed chunks out of the shirt and ripped a sleeve off, nearly yanking him in with it.

Another brief encounter with danger came when they passed a man who appeared to be intoxicated. He was sitting on the other side of the canal that overlooked a field. The man was shouting and whooping, waving a gun around and shooting it at random, supposedly at animals.

Jim was apprehensive, the memory of the man with the knife was too fresh. Jim kept Patty and Sam, riding her bicycle, right next to him. He was thankful the man wasn't paying any attention to them, but Jim was still afraid the man might swing around and take a shot at them. Jim was grateful when they were safely past the man. It had been a long, thirty-three mile day.

10 The City of the Golden Gate

SUNDAY, June 20. Father's Day.

Jim, Dotty, Patty, and Sam rested on a blanket under a comforting oak tree, while Granddad and Alfred napped in the camper. To keep themselves running when they were famished, Jim and Patty talked about everything but food. Now they were trying to talk about everything but the heat.

Their mental attitude was as critical to their running as their physical condition. Covering long distances day upon day in the hideous heat their minds begged their wills to surrender. Although their bodies longed to hibernate in a nice air-conditioned motel, they knew that yielding would destroy their mental fortitude and iron-willed tenacity.

Jim had lost his tolerance for the heat, and the long stretch on the canal had made him feel worse. They were waiting for the heat to diminish before running again. Dotty and the girls had given Father's Day gifts to Granddad and Jim, and the small celebration put Jim into a melancholy, reminiscing mood.

"You know, I never had the opportunity to call anybody Dad," he reflected. "We called almost everybody in my family by their names. My Grandmother is Nana, and my step-grandmother is Georgia. My stepfather was Chuck. I wasn't allowed to call my step-grandfather anything but Mr. Nelson.

"When I was a kid, I was really alone; I didn't have any brothers or sisters or a father." Jim looked at his daughters. "The biggest thrill in my life is when you girls and Richard call me Daddy or Dad." His voice broke, briefly. "That's the greatest Father's Day gift I could ever have."

"You never knew your dad?" Patty asked, astonished.

"I only met him once that I remember. I don't know how old I was, but I was at my Nana's house and my father sat me on the gasoline tank of his motorcycle and started to ride off. The weather was bad; I think it was raining. Nana was horrified and they quarreled. She wouldn't let me go with my father. When I was ten, he died from injuries in a motorcycle accident.

"I went from grandmother to grandmother and then finally to a boarding house," Jim continued. He wiped the sweat from his face and neck. "The Elizabeth Davis Home for Boys, it was called. I wanted to run away from that place. The only time I got out was on the weekends when my Mom would pick me up. It was just like getting out of prison. Of course, I didn't know what prison was like at that age. Every week she took me to the same restaurant and I had breaded veal cutlets and lemon meringue pie every Friday night for fifty-two weeks. I looked forward to it, probably because I kept hoping I would get sprung out of the boys' home. I hated it! I remember when we bathed. The lady was in there with you and she would scrub you down. It seemed like she used one of those hard brushes like you scrub . . ."

"The floor with!" exclaimed Dotty.

"Yes, and it always hurt. Then when I was in high school, I lived with my Nana and Mr. Nelson. But I hated high school, too, every minute of it from morning until night. That's why Buena Park High School is my high school. When you girls and Richard go to your classes and your teachers and your sporting events it's my school; I'm sharing in it. In my little fantasy world—and I fantasize all the time —you children are the brothers and sisters I never had. Our family is the family I didn't have. I'm constantly trying to live my life through your lives. People criticize me and say it's not right for me to live my life through my children. But I say to myself, even if they're right—and I don't know if they're right or not—I can't stop. I just love it!"

"You'd rather be with us than go to work," giggled Patty.

"When I was growing up, my ambition was to be a bum riding on the trains. I never conceived of the idea of being married and having a family."

"I never realized what it was like for you," Dotty said softly. "I had an extremely secure home. Dad worked at the post office until he retired. They moved into their house when I was two years old, and they're still living there."

"Mom, when did you meet Dad?" Sam asked.

"I was in high school and your father was in the Navy."

"I had a thirty-day leave after being stationed in Alaska. I had a red convertible and those sunglasses that are coated so that you can look out but no one can see your eyes. Anyway, my friend, Sydney, introduced us at Dorsey High School. I want to emphasize, girls, that your mother's name is *Dorothy Jean* Sturgis," Jim's eyes gleamed, "but later I changed it to Dotty. Your grandparents didn't like it because she was always Dorothy Jean. Anyway, I asked her for a date and said she could choose anyplace she wanted to go."

"I said that I like Chinese food," Dotty added. "We went to this Chinese restaurant in China Town."

"I'd never been there and I would *not* eat the food!" Jim continued. "Our date was absolutely disastrous. I didn't think much of her or our conversation. I loved sports, she didn't. No one in her family knew anything about sports. Zero! She loved to read books, I don't. I liked rock and roll music, she liked classical, semi-classical, and show music. She wanted to go to college, and I thought it was a waste of time. We had nothing in common. I brought her home that night. I thought, what a bomb!"

"It was horrible!" Dotty spoke soberly, but her eyes glistened. "His buddy called me and told me that he didn't think Dad was the right one for me. I'd lived a sheltered life and this was a Navy guy. Sydney told me I shouldn't see what's-his-name over there," Dotty gestured toward Jim.

"Two or three days later I called her up again and took her to the beach. But let me tell you, Patty and Sam, what a disaster! She took along a big book to read! I thought when you went to the beach it was to have fun, not sit and read a textbook or do homework. And the next thing she does, she jumps in the water and she swims almost to Catalina Island. She's out past the breakwater, almost past the pier, and she's wondering why I'm not out there, and the reason is I can't swim. But I'm not about to tell her."

"He still can't swim!" snickered Dotty.

"So when I took her home I just dropped her off. I told myself, I never want to see this girl again. I don't want to call her. I don't even want to remember her name or anything. Period. That was the end. The finish!"

"We didn't see each other for a week or so, that was it." said Dotty. "It was fine with me; I didn't want to see him again. Then he called me up. I don't know why and I don't even remember where we went after that, but everything clicked."

"I don't know why," Jim said with a boyish grin. "I loved blondes and she had dark hair. I loved girls with long hair, hers was short and curly. That's the second major change that upset her parents. I made her grow her hair real long and have it straightened. Now the curls have returned and she has short hair again. Anyhow, I loved the carefree, athletic type, but your mother was non-athletic, studious, the absolute opposite."

"Don't give me that wrinkled-nose grin. I didn't like your sort of boy, either!"

Patty's and Sam's eyes took on a soft glow as they watched their parents sharing their courtship, teasing back and forth, talking to them as if neither was present and each was talking to the girls alone.

"I was so proud of my red convertible. She didn't like it, because it messed up her hair, or it was too cold and we had to put the top up. There was no common ground, none, absolutely none! But here we are . . ."

"Still trying to find common ground!" finished Dotty. "But when he left for Germany, it was with the idea that we would get married. My parents wouldn't let me have an engagement ring, so he bought me a nice diamond watch."

"She broke up with me, though, while I was in Germany!"

"I told him I wanted to go to college. I didn't really break our engagement, but he felt it was as good as breaking it."

"I was really crushed! I was over there a year and four months. I played football on the Army team. The only reason we got together when I came back was that she was going to help me get into college on the G.I. bill. I was sure this egghead over here," Jim chuckled lovingly, "would know what to do. I might as well *use* her expertise!"

"I had my life going pretty well, and he showed up again. I'd become president of my sorority and was in the honor society. I was doing just fine! I was going to go to Europe after junior college."

"I offered her a chance to go to Europe, but she turned me down. If she had married me, we would have gone to Germany together."

"I was only seventeen!" Dotty protested. "I was nineteen when we did get married."

"She has no reason to complain. I'll tell you why, girls. I didn't have the two dollars to buy the marriage license, and that should have tipped her off. She had to buy it, so it's her doing. But your mother was a good choice," reflected Jim. "She's the hub of our family."

"My life has never been better!" Dotty smiled warmly. Jim hugged her and they fell back on the blanket laughing.

"Are you still out here?" Granddad Sturgis asked as he limped out of the camper.

"What time is it?" asked Jim.

"Three-thirty," he answered.

"Well, Patty, we'd better get moving if we're going to put in fifteen more miles today."

There always seemed to be new and unexpected obstacles. This afternoon the aqueduct had a "No Trespassing" sign posted, and a chain-link barbed wire fence and gate barred their entrance. But Jim was philosophical about everything, and was always challanged by the chance to conquer the impossible or forbidden.

"Daddy, we're not supposed to go through there!" Patty reminded her father.

"Life is made up of hurdles, Patty. They are constantly before us. We always have decisions to make. Do we turn back? Do we go around it? Or do we meet the challenge and go over it? I look at this obstacle as a hurdle. I'll be darned if we're going to let heat stop us, or personal trouble, or all those other things! Going over the mountain didn't stop us! Everyone thought it would. And I'm not going to let a little chain-link fence with barbed wire and a stupid sign stop us!"

"But, Daddy, I can't climb over it!"

"I'll lift the gate up and you whip underneath, then I'll climb over. It will take all the strength I have in my body, but I think I can lift it."

Patty slipped halfway under. "I can't go any farther. I'm stuck."

Jim was trying to get his thoughts together, to figure out how to get her out from underneath the gate. Without thinking, he released it and let it down on Patty.

"Dad . . . Dad . . . Dad . . . ," Patty gasped.

"Patty, be quiet! I'm trying to think how we're going to get through here."

"Dad . . . help me," she barely breathed the words.

"Patty! What do you want?"

"The fence . . . it's killing me."

Jim looked down and the whole huge gate was cutting his daughter in half, down the center of one breast, down her stomach and across one leg. She was turning gray. She couldn't take air in. The weight of the gate was cutting her oxygen off. Adrenaline rushed through Jim and gave him strength to lift the gate and let Patty escape. Fortunately, she wasn't injured, and they rested until she regained her breath. Then Jim lifted the gate again, Patty slipped under and then he climbed over.

Now they feared being caught by a sheriff from one of the small towns along the way, or by the planes that checked the waterways. Each time one flew down low to check for trespassers, Patty and Jim dropped to the ground to hide. There were also crop-dusting planes to duck.

Monday, Tuesday, and Wednesday were Patty and Jim's last and most peaceful days along the waterway. There had been luscious fruits to pick and eat, apricots and cherries, and one offensive garlic field. They had covered 173 miles along the waterways and were at the 372-mile mark, with only 128 more to the finish.

Dotty had returned home to go back to work. Twelve-year-old Sam would be responsible for caring for the runners' needs, doing the laundry and cooking, and keeping the log, in addition to biking and running with them. She added extra notes to the log about things that pleased her. "We seen a calico kitten . . . found a dog."

Patty was thankful to be off the aqueduct; she thought it was unbearably boring and hot. The exhaustion and the isolation had gotten to her. Meeting people along the way inspired her. She missed Richard, whom she hadn't been able to talk to the entire trip. She already missed her mother, the soothing link between Granddad and her father.

Mid-morning, Wednesday, they were on Highway 152, which would take them toward the coast. At two o'clock they quit and set up camp.

Patty decided Alfred, who refused to budge from the camper, should go for a run. When the dog saw a large lake near the campsite, he charged for it. Patty was hanging on to the leash, racing to keep pace with the dog. At the edge of the water, Patty sunk her feet in the mud, trying to hold Alfred back. The tainted lake smelled putrid, but that didn't seem to bother Alfred—he pulled Patty right out into it with him. She came up sputtering and reeking.

There were no showers at the campground, and Jim and Granddad had been fiddling with a homemade contraption—a hose and a bucket rigged for a shower. It was a crazy affair. Patty stood in the bucket while Jim and Granddad tried to get the shower working and hose the stench off Patty and her clothing. They all laughed and howled. It was a light moment Patty treasured, one that eased the serious tensions.

Over the next three days, critical fire danger continued to prevail from one end of California to the other because of the drought. US Forest Service officials, alarmed by such weather conditions so early in the season, issued a "red flag" warning and set up check points to caution visitors. They also warned that the dry conditions were expected to drive rattlesnakes out of the foothills.

When a rash of brush fires broke out, Jim watched the news nervously. They weren't near the fires, but the hellish, torrid weather continued to fatigue them, making them all irritable and edgy. He still had to chew antacids, even though they were starting

at midnight and running until daybreak. There was almost no relief
—sometimes the mercury dipped no lower than seventy-one degrees. Cars overheated and tires blew out, leaving fragments along
the highway. Pieces of fanbelts spooked Jim—in the darkness they
looked like rattlesnakes.

The mountain roads were more treacherous because semitruck
drivers didn't know Jim and Patty were out there. Several times they
had to pin themselves against the mountainside to escape mammoth
trucks whizzing by. They were afraid that the suction from the
wheels would pull them under the speeding trucks.

Those were the times Jim questioned his decision to have Patty
make this run. *We could become statistics in some county's morgue. Why
am I out here, exposing my daughter to these hazards?*

But there were also very special moments. At one campground
they met a boy from La Palma. They didn't know him, but it was
good to talk to someone from home. An older man, encouraged by
Patty's bravery, told her, "I didn't know young people still had the
pioneer spirit."

Once a man on his way to work passed Patty and Jim, and then
passed them again on his way home. He came back, aghast to think
they had been stranded all day, and offered them a ride. Even
truckers saluted them with a honk, after reading the sign on the
camper.

Unexpected, simple moments also brought them pleasure. Little
things like jack rabbits bounding away, a penny, a friendly horse, a
flower struggling through the pavement, or a precious puddle of
water exhilarated them. At other times they became aware of their
insignificance—two little people overshadowed by groves of tower-
ing trees and the endlessly changing landscape.

Flamboyant sunsets and soft sunrises gave them joy. They watched
respectfully as light saturated the velvet blackness, shooed the stars
away, turned the sky to shades of gray then pale blue. These poi-
gnant moments were like getting married or having your first child
or celebrating a silver anniversary, or a graduation.

Patty couldn't put all these impressions into words, but she knew
it was something her father and she were fortunate to have ex-

perienced. They could imagine what it must have been like for the first person who saw the Grand Canyon, the awe and the wonder of its majestic beauty. They knew how much greater the moment must have been if it had been shared with another person.

Running had developed a close bond between them, and they could read each other's thoughts most of the time. They answered each other in abbreviated sentences and played a question and answer game—usually about whether they wanted to go on another mile or two, or stop and take a break, or whatever might be happening at the time.

By Sunday, their seventeenth day, they were running across the San Francisco Peninsula in the suburb of Belmont. The eighteenth day found them in Milbrae, five miles from San Francisco's City Hall. Dotty had rejoined them, bringing Jim's Nana with her.

On the nineteenth day, June 29, 1976, Jim staged their final exhilarating five miles. He called reporters to inform them they would arrive at City Hall at eight o'clock in the morning. Patty and Jim slept restlessly their last night. It was like the excitement of waiting for Christmas morning.

They started at seven o'clock, dressed in matching red shorts and white T-shirts. Patty chattered to her father; she was nervous, anticipating the reception they would receive. Warm elation surged up in Patty. She wanted to hold on to it, yet it overwhelmed her.

A television camera crew and news photographers suddenly appeared and followed them down the street. Patty smiled for them uncomfortably.

Jim was excited, his hazel eyes twinkling. He watched his daughter with pride. He didn't think about this run in terms of something he'd accomplished; this was Patty's hour of glory. It was as if she'd run the 502.18 miles alone.

Their family, Dotty's brother and sister-in-law, Nana, Granddad Sturgis, and Walt Stack, president of the Dolphins Running Club, were waiting on the top of the steps at City Hall. They broke into cheers and applause when they spotted Patty and Jim in the distance.

Patty shyly waved in return. She was encouraged and pleased by the small but enthusiastic reception. She could feel her heartbeat accelerate, and she thought for a moment her excitement might consume her. Jim was wrestling with opposing emotions as he always did at a finale—the thrill of making it and the disappointment that their run was about to be over.

Patty reached out to take her father's hand; neither wanted to reach City Hall before the other. They quickened their pace, then dashed toward the steps. Their family and friends were clapping and yelling wildly.

On the portico at City Hall, a San Francisco supervisor presented Patty with a framed resolution by the Orange County Board of Supervisors, commending her feat. Patty and Jim and their family lingered, savoring this memory, while Dotty took pictures for their album.

That afternoon at Dotty's brother's home, Patty and Jim were thrilled to see themselves on television for the first time. They celebrated with dinner on Fisherman's Wharf and bought Patty a special memento, a tiny Golden Gate Bridge to add to her charm bracelet. Dotty and Sam had chalked up their own record. Dotty ran 20.75 miles and biked 32.76, while Sam ran twenty miles and biked 62.64.

The newspaper stories of Patty's record-breaking 502.18 mile ultra-marathon closed with the announcement of Jim's next goal: "One thousand miles to Portland, Oregon."

11   *Come Out of the Closet*

TO HONOR Patty's five-hundred-mile San Francisco feat, she was chosen to be a Junior Grand Marshal in La Palma's Fourth of July parade. She had run five times farther than any woman had ever run, but it was an unofficial world's record. To make it official, AAU representatives would have had to accompany the Wilsons on the trip, measuring every mile and following every step Patty ran.

Dotty had photographed the run and Sam and she had kept an exacting log of Patty's and Jim's mileage. He was meticulous about the running. They never walked if they tired; they stood in place or took a break. They ran every step, making sure they started and stopped in the same spot.

For the parade, Patty wore her candy striped shirt and white shorts. Tanned and confident, she smiled and waved to the people of their home town along the parade route. It was a proud moment for Jim and Dotty.

The parade was Patty's only breather. She had returned to cross-country training, and August first she competed in the 14.2 mile Pikes Peak Marathon in Colorado. There were five hundred marathoners, but Patty competed in the fourteen to nineteen age category against five other girls.

Patty ran most of the race in second place. She knew the girl who was in first, a nineteen year old who had already won a national cross-country race. Then Patty saw another girl pass, which meant Patty and Debbie, a friend from Buena Park High School, were vying for third. Patty knew where she stood; there was only one more medal she could win.

Should she stick with Debbie? She was shy and hadn't run a marathon before. Patty wrestled with her concern for her friend and her desire to win. She'd come a long way to get to the race, and if she didn't come back with anything she'd feel terrible. She wanted to win third! Friend, or not, she had to leave Debbie behind.

"Patty! Wait! Don't leave me!" her friend called.

"I can't stay back! I have to win!" Patty yelled and spurted ahead.

Patty ran the rugged, mountainous marathon in four hours and fifty-four minutes and won third place, receiving a bronze medal for her age category. Jim and she also won the silver medal for the father-daughter category. Winning a bronze medal at Pikes Peak and first place at the Santa Barbara Invitational gave Patty her greatest sense of achievement in her competitive running career.

When they returned home, Jim phoned local papers and told them about Patty's Pikes Peak accomplishment and used the opportunity to promote their Portland, Oregon, run. He added that they were planning a two thousand mile jaunt to St. Louis the following year, and a three thousand mile run across the United States when Patty graduated from high school.

Dotty, however, was strongly opposed to another long distance run. She had almost lost Jim to a heat stroke, and the strain had been too much. Nonetheless, Jim continued to talk up the Portland trip whenever he had the opportunity. Invariably, one of the first questions people asked Patty and him was, "Are you running for a cause?"

This repeated question peaked Patty's interest in the idea of running for charity. Although breaking her long distance record was important to her, she had powerful feelings about justice and fairness, equality and liberation. She had a heart for the special needs of special people. She collected door to door for different charities, and twice she had walked twenty miles for the March of Dimes.

Patty and Jim discussed the possibility, and one idea fed into another. Doubling her long-distance record would arouse the public's attention and provide publicity not only for her, but for a charitable organization. If they could persuade Dotty to agree to the Portland run, perhaps they could run for muscular dystrophy. They didn't consider epilepsy an option. Because it was a misunderstood closet disorder, they felt the risk that it might prejudice people against Patty was too great.

In the meantime, Patty was irritated by what she considered an extremely unfair situation. Several girls had started cross-country training season, but all had dropped out for various reasons. Now Patty was the only girl. It was almost time for Mammoth training camp. When the coach gave out the names of people who would be going, she was not among them.

Every night she'd drag in from practice and tell her parents, "I really don't think it's fair that all the guys can go to camp, and I can't because I'm a girl!"

At first Jim and Dotty tried to placate Patty, thinking it impossible for her to go. Then they heard about Title Nine, which implied that, girls with equal ability on the same team should have the same treatment.

Jim called a conference with the coach, who argued, "Patty would be the lone girl with twenty boys. You never know what might happen!"

"Fine," countered Jim. "Patty can handle herself."

"There are no showering facilities for women," the coach explained.

"She can shower before or after the boys," suggested Jim.

After a half hour, Patty was dismissed from the meeting. She waited anxiously outside while Jim and the coach contested the camp issue. It seemed to Patty that the debate went on for another three hours. When her father came out, Patty knew the decision by the triumphant expression on his face. She was going to camp.

High altitude and mountainous terrain made Mammoth a rugged area for a conditioning camp. The workouts were more strenuous than Patty anticipated, but she felt she'd asked for it when she wanted to go to camp; she determined to keep up with the program. Speed was still not her forte, and during one race with another high school, she got lost because she didn't know the course. She was last, and none of the other runners were in sight when she came to a fork in the road. She had no idea which road to take, so she stopped where she was and waited for someone to find her.

Coach, please come pick me up, she begged silently. *I'm sorry! I hope you won't be mad at me, but please come get me. I'm lost and I don't know* *where to go. Please come pick me up,* she repeated, to assure herself that she would be rescued.

The coach was logging in the guys and their times, and the last one straggled in at thirteen minutes. he said, "When it hits twenty we'll go out and look for her."

After they found her, the guys razzed Patty. "The course was so simple! How could you get lost?"

Patty was too embarrassed to admit that her eyes couldn't keep up with the bends and turns and hills. She had no sense of direction. The year before she had become lost in the mountains during a Patriots' training camp.

The guys enjoyed teasing her, but they accepted her as one of them. Evenings they listened to nighttime theatre on the radio. The boys had regular sized tents, but Patty's was a pup tent. She thought it was terribly inconvenient to crawl in and out. After the guys settled into their sleeping bags, they'd ask Patty if she wanted to come inside with them and listen to the radio. She declined; she enjoyed sitting outside on the ground, leaning against one of their suitcases, listening to the programs.

The mysterious sounds of the night didn't frighten her. A breeze strumming pine needles played a quiet lullaby for her. The stars winked and the black sky had a clarity that the smog screened out at home. She giggled at the boys' laughter and crazy pranks. The boys goofing around, the radio theatre, and the fragrance of pine and sounds of the night were a generous gift to Patty. She cherished those special moments.

An epidemic of summer colds swept through the team. Patty missed a few workouts, but she had determined to run every day. No matter how sick she was, she ran. She felt an edge of pride at the fact that some of the guys only ran three days out of the entire two weeks, while she hadn't missed a day. Because so many of the team were ill, they finally returned home a day early.

In the fall, school became Patty's second home, even though her dream eluded her: she wasn't selected to be a cheerleader. But Patty still thrived on activities, and the busier she was, the happier she was.

She was Girl's Athletic Association Vice-President, and there were cross-country meets, Friday night football games, dates, and dances. During cross-country season there were a few girls' races, but most of them didn't count toward anything. For example, in one particular race the boys received medals, but the girls were not awarded any, which upset Patty. At the end of the season she finished fourth in league against girls from other high schools. Next, she played on the girls' hockey team.

But her busy schedule could not hide the inner pressure of the great secret Patty felt she had kept hidden for so long. There were a few people who knew she had epilepsy, but she believed the majority did not know. Certain ideas were taking shape in her mind —thoughts about the way people with epilepsy were treated, the way she had been treated.

In her sophomore year, something happened to crystalize Patty's feelings and to challenge her thoughts. The drama unfolded like a four-act play. The first scene played in her classroom almost daily.

"Are you all right, Patty?" the teacher asked. "Do you feel like you're going to have a seizure?"

"I'm just tired," Patty explained again.

Patty propped her textbook up to block her face from the teacher. *Why do you have to ask me in front of the class?* she fumed to herself. *Can't you believe me? I'm tired. I keep telling you I'm doing a lot of activities. Can't you understand that?* Patty wanted to shout. *This is a solid subject. It's after lunch! It's hot! Everybody's tired, not just me. Are they going to have a seizure? Why not ask them?"*

Every day Patty fought to stay alert. She dared not look the least bit tired, or the teacher would panic and ask, "I know you're on medication. Are you okay?"

It was difficult for Patty, because her seat was in front and there was no one to hide behind. One afternoon, Patty was especially bored. The teacher's voice droned on and on, and Patty drifted off. Without thinking, she laid her head down on the desk. The teacher stopped in midsentence.

"Are you okay?" she exclaimed, rushing to Patty's desk. "Are you going to have a seizure?"

Patty jerked upright. "I'm tired!" she snapped, stifling her impulse to scream. "You're boring me to death!"

"This protection's driving me crazy!" Patty complained to her parents. Actually, she felt humiliated, embarrassed, and betrayed. The most important secret of her whole life was being broadcast to everyone. She was close to tears and furious. Why was the teacher so scared? Patty hadn't had had a seizure in class since sixth grade.

Whenever Jim and Dotty met this teacher, whether in a group or in a private conference, she started the conversation with the same tired phrase: "I know Patty has a medical problem . . ."

Dotty recognized that the teacher was overreacting. Perhaps she feared she wouldn't know how to handle it if Patty had a convulsion in her class. None of Dotty's assurances seemed to calm the teacher. Finally Dotty told Patty, "The teacher's just uptight. Grit your teeth and you'll get through the year."

The second act started with an encounter Patty had with a counselor. There was a special health-needs team assigned to students with physical handicaps. Patty's counselor called her in periodically to ask how she was doing.

Patty always felt as if she had to tell the counselor, "I'm doing fine!"

If she told them she needed help with a subject she didn't understand, they would provide a tutor. The one time she had asked for help had been too degrading. Patty was slightly above average in her grades, but they treated her as if she were a kindergartener. Patty thought the special help was a fine concept, but not the way it seemed to be handled. She wasn't used to receiving a negative reaction to her "handicap," and wondered what happened to people who constantly experienced this sort of treatment. How did they survive?

Her parents treated her normally, expecting no less from her because she had epilepsy, or treating her any differently than Richard or Sam. If anything, they challenged her to do the extraordinary, to prove to herself she was capable.

Now she felt like her epilepsy was a malicious ghost, darting around corners, appearing unexpectedly, following her everywhere, carrying a banner which proclaimed: "Be careful! This girl has seizures!"

The third scene opened in winter, during second semester in a different classroom. The teacher was answering questions. Patty was listening intently, when her attention was drawn to a tall boy standing next to the teacher. Something seemed to be wrong; the boy had a distressed, puzzled expression, a lost look about him that was strangely familiar. A slight fever of fear flushed Patty.

The boy leaned over the teacher, who was much shorter than he. The teacher started to shrug the boy off, but when he did the entire weight of the boy's body fell against him. The boy's face was gray; his eyes stared blankly. He looked wretched.

Patty watched the teacher struggling to hide his fear, but a hysterical note in his voice betrayed him. He wrestled the boy on to a chair.

Patty felt unusually tense and oddly shaken. She remembered her father's description of a seizure she had once had. She had been running to Bellis Park with her father when suddenly she turned gray and stopped running. Her father said she had looked dead. So did this boy. The way he acted before he passed out and the way he looked now were exactly what her father had described.

But that was different. She wasn't conscious then, and she hadn't seen herself. Except for what Jim had told her, she couldn't even recall what she had done or how she had acted. Watching the boy was much worse than having a seizure. It was horrible! She was seeing a reflection of herself, of what she might have looked like in third grade when she had a convulsion. This is how the children had probably reacted! Patty fought to control a blind, unreasoning panic.

She could hear herself talking, chanting in a monotone, "Lay him down. Lay him down. Lay him down." Her voice was usually so loud it carried, but she was whispering. It was all she could do. She couldn't move, still she had an overwhelming urge to run away from the situation.

"Uuhhh, he looks awful!" she heard someone gasp. She could feel the repulsion around her. Her alarm grew; she hadn't told anyone in the room she had epilepsy. She knew that some people were aware of it, but she had never had to confess it to them. If they did know, they never talked to her about it; maybe they discussed it behind her back.

She felt like a curious spectator who had rushed to the scene of an accident and stayed among the crowd to gawk. It made her sick. She couldn't stand watching what was happening, and she was overpowered by a desperate desire to escape.

"We need a wheelchair," she heard the teacher request above the confusion swirling and dancing around her.

"I'll go!" She had regained her voice; it was high and excited.

Patty was up before anyone else could respond. She darted out the door and sprinted down the walk. She knew she was more than reasonably upset. She was thankful to be free and grateful that their class was at the back corner of the campus, a long distance from the main office.

When she picked up the wheelchair, she dashed back to the room with it. Running siphoned some of her terror. After the young man was wheeled out, the class settled down again. Patty thought everyone seemed too eager to return to work. She couldn't; she felt half gone. She was deeply weary, spent of all energy and feeling.

The boy was absent several days, and when he returned Patty couldn't make herself speak to him or look at him. She avoided him. She was still afraid. She couldn't ask him how he was doing. If they both had epilepsy, they had something to share. She felt awkward and ashamed, and she couldn't for the life of her talk to him.

The fourth and final act happened that spring in Patty's health class. The students were assigned a report on a major disease. When Patty saw the list of choices and she came across the word *epilepsy,* a weird, cold feeling cut through her.

At first she thought she'd choose anything but epilepsy. She'd choose a disorder she could discuss safely, objectively. If she talked to them about epilepsy, someone would know she had it. She wouldn't be able to conceal it. The fear in her eyes or an off-note in her voice would give her away. Maybe she could borrow a film from the Orange County Epilepsy Society and show it? That might be safer.

But she was distressed by distorted images of the boy, a fresh, painful presence that stood at the edge of her consciousness. She argued with herself, trying to reason away her irrational feelings. The boy was a real person; he wasn't acting for a film. He was out of control for the moment. It was something he could not help. The teacher could only go through the motions of taking care of him and then let him rest, just as her family did whenever she had a seizure. What happened to him, happened to her. She shouldn't be agitated about it.

Showing a film would be different; it wouldn't be so personal. She began to feel more comfortable about the movie. As the idea matured in her mind, she felt very strongly about the class seeing it. She wanted them to know what it was like to have a convulsion, and what they should do if they ever witnessed one.

The day of the film she briefly considered revealing that she had epilepsy. Then, when the person on the screen had a convulsion, Patty heard a quiet ripple. "Oooo!" "Ugh!" There was a crescendo of words. "Ohhh, how ugly!" "Yuck!" "That's gross!" In the flickering light she could see the students turning away, closing their eyes, or hiding behind their fingers, peeking out to see if it was over. No, she could not tell them she had epilepsy. Never!

When the movie was over and the lights went on, Patty disguised her anxiety. She had extraordinary control over her emotions, when she needed to. She smiled her warm lovely smile as she passed out pamphlets about epilepsy. When she sat down she was numb, but no one would have guessed she was distressed. She laughed and joked as usual, as if she had no connection to the film. She was never more thankful to hear the bell ring; class had ended. If only she could bury herself somewhere and cry.

The four-act play was over, but Patty couldn't continue to hide from the critics. Something was stirring inside her—someone had to write a new script for this play.

If she told people she had epilepsy, she might receive their pity. She abhorred the thought! On the other hand, she couldn't deal with the unthinking reaction and repulsion people expressed when they witnessed a seizure. What would they have done if she had had the convulsion?

The fervor spread inside her and refused to leave her alone. It confronted her, pressed in on her, and demanded an answer. She wanted people to have a more compassionate, accepting view of epilepsy and the people who had it. Respect and dignity. It always returned to that.

The more Patty brooded over it and the more she remembered the four-act play, the more worked up she became. Epilepsy—changing its image, bringing it out, proving that people with epilepsy are normal and lead ordinary lives—this mattered more than anything to Patty. It became her passion. She asked her Dad if they could run for epilepsy. they could announce that she had it when they advertised their Portland send-off date.

Dotty, however, continued to object to the Oregon trip, and they knew they couldn't do it without her. Although it had been almost ten months since the San Francisco run, Dotty argued that Jim was still too sensitive to the sun. When he was out in it he had to chew antacid tablets to control the nausea. Dotty had to watch him constantly. When he was running, she'd insist that he wear a hat. Otherwise, he would become sicker faster.

It was hard on Jim's ego to think that the time when he could stand extreme heat was past. Dotty and Patty were forever reminding him, "Don't forget your hat!" "Daddy, I don't want you to get too much sun." Jim didn't like it; it was a chink in his armor.

He wasn't convincing Dotty, and there were other skeptics who advised him against attempting the Oregon trip. The more opposition Jim encountered, the more determined he was that Patty and he could do it. He would prove them wrong! His every moment was dedicated to planning Patty's and his future. Jim's dreams had become Patty's dreams and together they urged Dotty to change her mind. Finally, she was persuaded.

But Jim and Dotty were torn and reluctant about announcing to the public that Patty had epilepsy. They thought raising money and helping a charity was a terrific idea, but this was different. They understood the repercussions. The grandparents on both sides were worried and opposed to it. It wasn't proper. It would disgrace the family. It would ruin Patty's life. It would destroy her future. She wouldn't be able to find a job. Jim feared she'd be stopped from competing in marathons. Her running days would be over.

It was an awesome risk, an irreversible decision. Once it was aired publicly it could never be denied. Patty persisted, she wanted it revealed. It wasn't a risk for her anymore; it was a great opportunity to do what she felt she should.

First, Jim contacted the Orange County Epilepsy Society and discussed it with them to see if they would be interested. They reacted with great excitement. Usually people called for information. When people found out that they or someone in their family had epilepsy, they either would not reveal their names or would request that their identities be kept a secret. Often, the epilepsy society heard from people once, then never heard from them again.

Jim began to admit his own deep feeling about Patty's epilepsy and faced his fears. When Patty was in sixth grade and he had been told she had epilepsy, he was afraid of the word. He didn't know what it was or what it meant. He just knew it must be something like having leprosy or polio. He put Patty's epilepsy in a safe compartment labled *denial,* where it stayed until she had a seizure. Jim hadn't started Patty running because she had epilepsy, but because he was going to help his clumsy little girl.

One month before the Portland, Oregon send-off, Jim and Dotty finally agreed with Patty to announce she was running for a disorder that she had kept secret. Jim called Frances Pinkert of the *Daily News Tribune.*

The headlines of Thursday, May 19, 1977 read "Handicap No Barrier For Girl on Run." Next to the caption was a picture of Patty tying her shoe. Her eyes crinkled with a hint of budding mischief, and her wide smile tugged at the corners of her cheeks in a radiant, triumphant expression.

When she was asked, "Was your decision to 'come out of the closet' made for the purpose of grandstanding?" Patty answered instantly.

"I think it will help other people who have epilepsy if they know. If they don't know I have it and see me running, they say, 'That's nice.' But if they know I've got epilepsy, they might figure, 'Wow, maybe I can do something like that!' I want something to come out of these runs. Maybe they'll bring some good for somebody else."

Patty mentioned another long-range goal of hers. She hoped the power of a public statement might be enough push to rectify the quality of the male-dominated cross-country league. "I'm looking forward to this Portland trip but also I'm looking past it because I want to do well in cross-country. We're hoping to have an official girls' cross-country league next year!"

Jim also admitted his apprehensions, "For a long time we were reluctant for her to be frank about this because we were afraid Patty would be ridiculed or harmed in some way. But she reached the decision on her own. She didn't want this to be kept secret. She wants to face it. To be honest with herself. We've come to the conclusion it's a healthier situation not to hide."

The pressures and needs of a run of this magnitude were rushing in. While seeking sponsors, Jim and Patty had been training 125 miles each week. One evening at sunset they were running shoulder to shoulder. The lane narrowed to a single aisle and Jim burst up the hill ahead of Patty. When he turned to look back, Patty had disappeared.

12 *Run with the Light*

IT WAS that brilliant, blinding hour before sunset. Jim was standing at the top of an overpass. The bumper-to-bumper traffic screeched to a halt then clamored on, clogging the freeway below, infecting the already irritated air with fumes. Jim shielded his eyes with his hands and searched the landscape for Patty.

Before they left home, he had gone over the new route he planned to run with Patty. He had rehearsed it with her. She hadn't wanted to take it, because it meant going up a hill. Did she take their usual course? He wasn't sure, but he really didn't think so. The first stirrings of worry nagged him.

He swooped back down the hill and scouted the area. When he came back to where he'd started up the hill, he remembered the gas station—she had probably stopped to use the restroom like she usually did. Jim darted across the street and asked the attendants if they had seen Patty. He described her carefully, but they hadn't seen her.

Jim covered their regular loop down Valley View, to La Palma, then down to Walker and on to home. When Jim burst into the family room, Richard was stretched out on the couch watching television. He hadn't seen Patty.

Jim flew back to Orangethorpe, to Valley View, and on to where he had lost Patty. He dashed up the hill, but she wasn't anywhere in sight. He came back down and crossed over to the gas station again, then continued on, stopping to ask bicyclists and anyone along the street, "Have you seen a little girl run by here?" He described her, her clothing, and showed them how tall she was by measuring her height against his chest.

No one had seen her. Now Jim was genuinely alarmed. He turned and fled home. Dotty was waiting out front for him, and they scrambled into the car and drove through their tract. Jim wished it weren't so dark. Only a few porch lights and street lamps shone in the blackness.

All the reasons Jim had been given not to let Patty run screeched at him like witches. *A girl with epilepsy has no business running! A girl shouldn't run cross-country. There are molesters out there! A van could pull up and a couple of guys could open the side doors, grab her, overpower her, and throw her inside. She could be raped! She could be murdered and her body dumped somewhere. You'd never see her again!*

Jim was a prisoner of these horrid fears. He fought to free himself, to think of something else, but he continued to interrogate himself mercilessly. *Where was Patty? What if she were abducted? What would they do to her? Maybe she was just mad at me and took off. She wouldn't run away! What if she had a seizure? What if she was hit by a car? She can't . . . she can't be lying dead somewhere!* The urgency of the situation suffocated him and he slumped against the wheel of the car and tried to drive and concentrate on searching for Patty.

Dotty scanned every dark niche, while Jim and she questioned each other about places where Patty might have disappeared. Jim inched over every route they usually ran together until Dotty and he exhausted all possibilities.

They checked at home, but no Patty. They drove the streets again, but they still couldn't find Patty. Jim felt as if his heart were pounding in his mouth. "I hate doing it, but do you think we should call the police?"

"We don't have any other choice," Dotty answered, trying to restrain her intense fear.

When they reached Walker and were turning into their tract, they spotted Patty running toward them. She turned the corner without seeing them and headed for home. Jim sped around the corners to their street, sprung out of the car, and raced back toward her.

"Where have you been?" he exploded, yelling at her as she started down the street. "What have you been doing? Do you know your mother and I have been out of our minds?" he cried hysteri-

cally. Beads of perspiration covered him and he clenched and un-
clenched his fists, trying to control his rage. He wanted to grab Patty
and shake her, yet he was relieved. He had found her and she was
safe.

"Where were you?" he demanded. "Don't you realize . . ."

Patty looked up at him uncertainly, her child's eyes bewildered.
Her distressed expression asked, *Why is Daddy upset with me? Why
is he yelling at me?*

Grief and a painful tenderness, rose up in Jim. He was upset with
himself, at his anger and his ignorance. It was clear to him that Patty
had had a seizure. He tried to gain control of himself so he wouldn't
frighten her, to see if she could piece together where she had been
and what had happened to her.

"Patty, where did you go?" he asked gently, "Do you remember?"

"Well, where did *you* go?" Patty finally asked, but she was obvi-
ously still confused.

Impulsively, Jim hugged her, cradling her in his arms. He was
close to tears. How could he understand what was going on as far
as her seizures, her epilepsy? He wasn't an expert. He wasn't the
doctor; he was a parent. He'd fallen off the wall and he was breaking
into a thousand pieces.

Later that evening, they were able to put the story together. Patty
had been talking to Jim when they got to the bottom of the hill, but
she wasn't aware that her father had turned and sprinted up the hill.
She had continued down Orangethorpe toward Bellis Park and all
this time—about a mile and a half—she was talking to Jim even
though he wasn't there. Finally she reached the park. They had run
to it so many times, instinct had taken her there.

"When I started to come out of it a little bit," Patty spoke wistfully. "I didn't know where I was. I didn't know where you were,
Daddy . . . ," her voice faltered, ". . . I didn't even remember if you
had been with me. So I sat on a bench for a long time and waited.
I guess I thought you'd come get me. I felt completely lost." Patty
paused and closed her eyes for a moment. "Something inside me
must have told me to come home."

"You crossed the busy streets without knowing if the lights were green or red?" Jim's eyes searched hers.

"I don't know," Patty wrinkled her brow. "I'm not sure. I really didn't start coming out of it until I saw you and Mom."

Jim gasped. "Oh, Patty! This is worse than if you were a victim of amnesia."

It took Dotty and Jim several hours before the emotional shock started to wear off. Patty was tired and still not completely aware of what had happened. A night's sleep and she would be herself again, never really experiencing the terror her parents had felt.

Jim retreated into self-questioning, into agony and fear about Patty running and about her safety. He had known he had to stay close to her, but she had become lost anyway. He couldn't think about it. He would watch her, that was all.

By morning they were all cast into the chaos of their Portland trip; their hectic schedule seemed to propel them on. Jim and Patty continued their rugged training routine, day upon day without a break. Patty was running mornings, at school, and at home evenings. Even when she had Friday night dates, there was no sleeping in on weekends. Jim and she were up early, running fifteen miles to her favorite place, the beach.

She was running girls' track and her coach had her competing in every event. She was coming in third and fourth in the 880, and second and third in the mile and two mile. She would compete in a hard race, then sometimes put in nine more miles afterwards, because Jim felt they needed to have fifteen in for the day. Jim and she ran mountainous terrain to prepare for Highway One, a hairpin curved, hilly route. They were racing up and down mountains, and it was so tough they would be sick when they were through.

It was already May and their target day, June 18, was closing in. The nitty-gritty details of planning a trip of this magnitude were overwhelming. Jim not only sold insurance, but he sold others on this latest adventure. Bob Bradach, a friend and client, became so excited about what they were doing that he asked his company if he could devote all of his time to managing the Wilson's run. The

Porvene Company agreed to let Bob assist the Wilsons, and added that they would be one of the sponsors. The expenses of the trip were well beyond the Wilsons' income.

Bob had taken over the responsibility of locating a self-contained recreational vehicle—it was time for Granddad's trusty camper to retire. Bob also contacted every chamber of commerce in every city Jim and Patty planned to run through, asking them to support the run and telling them they were raising money for epilepsy organizations along their route.

The Orange County Epilepsy Society arranged for the Epilepsy Center of Oregon to take care of details of publicizing and safely routing the Wilsons through the state. John Baker was appointed to be in charge of public relations in Oregon, and Bob would coordinate in California.

In the brief span of a month, Bob organized the entire run and a multitude of "run Patty run" promotional activities. A reporter from NBC news and two cameramen filmed Patty and Jim during one of their workouts, and came to one of Patty's track sessions at the high school for a special news spot.

Wednesday, June 8, Patty threw out the first baseball at Anaheim's Angel Stadium. The giant scoreboard spelled out her story, announcing her mission and that she had epilepsy.

Saturday, June 11, exactly seven days before the send-off, Patty ran in the twenty-six mile Palos Verdes Marathon again. This time she finished before the final hour was up, but she didn't place. Then she was rushed to a fair in Fountain Valley for a brief live interview on the *Saturday* television show.

Sunday, June 12, Patty and her family were guests of Dr. Robert Schuller, pastor of Garden Grove Community Church. Jim had been inspired by a series of Dr. Schuller's messages on striving to reach a goal, and had invited him to give the invocation at their send-off. Patty's courage, in turn, inspired Dr. Schuller and he televised an interview with her for a nationwide segment of his *Hour of Power* program.

To publicize her Portland trip, Bob Bradach organized a six-mile mini-marathon for one o'clock, immediately after her appearance on

Hour of Power, and invited hundreds of runners to come out and run with her.

The activity was exhilarating for Dotty, who loved being a part of the show as long as she didn't have to be on stage. Along with the great excitement, there were the pressures and frustrations of working her regular shifts at the hospital, trying to buy the necessary provisions, and arranging for Richard, who had elected to stay home and work. Dotty was torn between looking forward to the run and not wanting to leave her son behind.

On Tuesday, June 14, the worst happened again. Jim and Patty had just run up and over the freeway overpass. The smoggy air irritated their eyes and choked their breathing. Patty was trying to tell Jim a story.

"Mrs. . . . you know who I mean. . . . I can't remember what I was . . ." Patty stopped in the middle of the sidewalk. Jim was just ahead of her, glancing back and listening. She stood staring as if hypnotized, her arms and legs fixed in a running position. She couldn't speak at all. Jim noticed her breathing was shallow, although she had just run three miles and her chest should have been heaving up and down. She was having a seizure!

Jim took Patty by the hand and led her to the curb. He sat her down next to him and went through his usual routine of questions, trying to bring her out of it. But she just stared at him, uncomprehending. He played his finger game, holding up different fingers, trying to get her to match the same one. It was about thirty minutes before she came around.

He asked her, "Are you okay?"

When she answered, he felt as if he were hearing her say her first word. "Fine," she said simply.

"Do you want to continue?"

"Yes."

They started to complete the last three miles home, but she retreated into the same trance-like state. Her breathing was shallow, but she was running. Now she was a little tin soldier, her arms swinging stiffly and her legs marching up and down.

"Patty! Patty speak to me," Jim pleaded. "Honey, answer me.

Please say something! Anything! Just let me know you hear me."
But Patty didn't answer Jim. She didn't even look at him. She
stared straight ahead, yet she was able to run without tripping on the
curbs. Jim ran on the outside to protect her and they continued for
two miles. He couldn't get over it; she was absolutely out.

A mile before they got home something clicked on again and she
smiled and said, "Hi, Daddy!"

"Hi, Pat." Jim was suddenly overcome by the strain of watching
the one he loved lost to him in a never-never land. It was terrible
and frightening and he was tired.

After a seizure, Patty was generally exhausted. That evening she
picked at her meal. Too weary to eat, she went to bed and slept
twelve hours. Even her sleep concerned Jim and Dotty, for she was
in an unwakeable "Snow White" sleep. Before Jim went to bed, he
checked on her; her pajamas were damp with perspiration, her long
hair flowed over her pillow, her arms and legs curled and tangled
in her sheets and blanket. Jim's emotions overpowered him. She
seemed so childlike, so innocent, and tears threatened to stream
down his cheeks.

He was fighting again with that old accusation: *What right do I have
to let Patty run?* Jim knew he would have to watch Patty, just as he
always had. He couldn't see why she had to give up something she
wanted to do just because she had seizures. She would have them
even if she didn't run.

He was already sparring with the doomsday prophets, as he called
them, who kept telling him that Patty and he could never run one
thousand miles, that what he was proposing was insanity, and that
they would never make it up Highway One.

Jim thought about all the phone calls Patty had received, and
about the parents of children with epilepsy. He thought about how
much he loved Patty and how much they loved their children and
wanted them to participate in sports and school activities, have jobs,
and live normal lives. He questioned whether it might be more
demoralizing for Patty to give up because she had an almost overwhelming, frightening handicap. Wouldn't it be better to let her
taste victory? To prove to others and to herself that she didn't have

to hide in a closet just because some people believe that's where people with handicaps belong?

Strangers had been calling ever since Patty's epilepsy was made public. Jim was touched when people came up to him and shyly asked if they could meet his daughter, or if she would talk to their daughter, or son, or grandson, or niece. "Do you think it would be possible sometime?" they asked. "I don't mean now; I know you're busy because of your trip. But it would mean so much to my child, because he has epilepsy too."

Someone sent them a five dollar check in honor of a family member who had epilepsy. Others wrote to say what a wonderful, brave thing Patty was doing, and they wished they would have done it, but they never had the courage.

Often when people phoned Patty, they were more interested in her epilepsy than in the fact that she planned to run a thousand miles. Jim often found her talking excitedly on the phone.

"Who are you talking to now?"

"I don't know," Patty mouthed, holding her hand over the receiver. "I can't even say the lady's name." She spelled it out and it was Oriental. "I can hardly understand her, but her son has epilepsy and I'm talking to her," beamed Patty.

Late one night, Patty was chatting on the phone when Jim came in. "Are you talking to Debbie again?" he scowled.

"No!" she shook her head, and held up her hand as a sign that she needed more time.

"Five more minutes!" he signed back, holding up five fingers. "And that's all!"

When Jim checked on her twenty minutes later she was still talking. "Patty!" he scolded. "Get off the phone!"

"Just a minute, Daddy!" she waved him off.

When Jim finally pulled Patty away, she protested, "But Daddy! I was talking to this boy from Servite High School. He's coming over to see me. He has epilepsy, too, and he's never had anyone his age he could talk to about it. He runs track like me. And we were discussing our medications and the problems we have."

"That's nice Patty! I'm glad you're doing that, but the ABC televi-

Patty begins her 2,000 mile run from Minneapolis to Washington, D.C. Among the runners accompanying Patty on the first few miles of the Super Run are, from left, Joe Frazer, regional vice-president of Family Weekly *magazine; Gov. Rudy Perpich (in back); Jim Autry, EFA president; Jim Wilson; and (far right) Rep. Albert Quie.* (UPI photo)

As the Super Run reaches Chicago, Patty is joined by Mayor Bilandic (on her right), who accompanies her through the city.
(Photo courtesy EFA)

Patty joins Mrs. Carter on the platform at a reception in Rochester, New York, in honor of Patty's Super Run. (Photo courtesy EFA)

In New York, Patty is joined for a few of the 2,000 miles by Susie Berge, who was a national poster child for the Epilepsy Foundation of America. (Photo courtesy EFA)

Patty and Jim break through the finish line in Washington, D.C., at the close of the 2,000 mile run. (Photo courtesy EFA)

A triumphant moment at the completion of the Super Run. (In background from left: Patty's grandparents, who flew in specially for the finale, Dotty, Jim, Jack McAllister, executive director of EFA, Al Rosso, Washington, D.C., government official, Governor Jerry Apodaca of New Mexico, chairman of the President's Council on Physical Fitness, and Jim Autry, president of EFA.) (Photo courtesy EFA)

sion crew and some newspaper reporters are coming to our house tomorrow morning. You need your sleep! Now get to bed!"

"Oh, Daddy. Do I have to? You know I don't like to talk to them."

"Patty, how many kids would love to be on television or have their pictures in the paper or have stories written about them? I have a philosophy about all this. I believe some things in life are scheduled to happen. You don't have any control over them. Perhaps you're destined to be a part of something great. You could become a symbol; the one to break the prejudices against epilepsy. You could become a star!"

"I like talking to people one to one," Patty sighed. "I feel like I'm helping them. That's what I want to do when I grow up—help people. But I hate the interviews! I feel funny. I'm embarrassed. I never know what to say to the reporters. Someone's always sticking a dumb microphone in my face. They ask me so many questions, I don't know what to say and I freeze up!"

"You'll get over it one of these days. You won't even give it a second thought."

Patty shrugged. How could she tell him how she really felt? She had been jostled and swirled from current to current down a raging river of activities and appearances. She was exhausted by them and wished she were on the road, running alone with her father.

By Wednesday, June 15, Bob had secured a deluxe vehicle, a twenty-two-foot motor home. The ABC news crew taped a segment to be shown on the evening news.

Thursday, June 16, Patty had been invited to the dugout at Dodger Stadium. She threw out the ball and was thrilled to meet the players, especially thrilled to talk to Don Sutton.

Friday, June 18, 1977. Send-off morning. The family was dressed by five o'clock, even though the ceremonies didn't start until nine at the Buena Park Mall. The grandparents were already there, along with Pete Strudwick, the footless runner who had first inspired them, and a host of other friends. It was like a circus; people were all over the lawn and in the garage. Cars lined Redwood Circle. Filled with nervous energy, people milled back and forth trying to organize themselves. It was next to impossible.

Bob Hickey and some others, charged with excitement, were chanting, "Let's go! Let's go! Let's go!"

When they arrived at the mall, they were met by television crews and people who wanted to give Patty shoes and running shorts. Microphones were thrust at her, and a roar of questions came from every direction.

When the hour finally arrived, the ceremonies began with a flair. The hundred member Cavalier band opened with the theme from *A Chorus Line.*

Patty and Jim appeared to be listening intently to an array of speeches by sportsmen and city, county, and state politicians. Pete Strudwick spoke a tribute. Patty received a California flag, other gifts, and a proclamation commending her to the Governor of Oregon. A representative from the California Epilepsy Society said, "She is demonstrating that people with epilepsy can do what everyone can do and then some!" She was given the *Candle of Understanding,* symbol of the Epilepsy Foundation of America, to carry.

Dr. Robert Schuller read his *Possibility Thinkers Creed,* which was inscribed on a medallion he presented to Patty. "When faced with a mountain I WILL NOT QUIT! I will keep on striving until I climb over, find a pass through, tunnel underneath or simply stay and turn the mountain into a gold mine, with God's help."

No one could have known at that moment how significant this creed would become for Patty and her family. No one could have known that a serious injury would almost destroy their run, and that these words would inspire Patty to go on.

Patty and Jim had talked for weeks about how they would start off. They agreed they wouldn't race out like they had in the past; they'd run slowly, so the other runners could keep pace with them. But the ceremonies were going on and on and their adrenalin was flowing through them, building up electricity. They hadn't eaten a thing. They were anxious to start, but they tried to be polite through the long ceremony.

Finally the program was over, and the Cavalier band formed into a marching unit. Dressed in white feather-plumed buccaneer hats and dashing red, white, and black uniforms, they led the crowd to the take-off point. Some of the band members, as well as the runners and even Patty's grandparents, were wearing bright blue "run Patty run" T-shirts.

Fifteen-year-old Patty, five feet four, solid and tanned, was lost among the almost all male runners who were going to run the first few miles with her. To keep her waist-length hair from blowing in her face, she had tied it with a band. Her gold barrettes and the medallion swinging from her neck glistened in the sunlight. She was wearing kelly green striped shorts and a blue tank top that advertised her run. Poised and tense, she stood shifting from foot to foot.

She sprang forward at the signal, saluting the red ribboned candle in the air. She tore through the paper banner just ahead of her father. She turned to the crowd and waved, then raced out of the parking lot, down La Palma Street followed by a colorful parade of police motorcycles, cars, and runners.

By the time Patty and Jim reached the fifteen-mile mark, they were down to five runners. A paramedic crew had accompanied them in case any runner passed out. When they stopped for a break, the attendants gave Patty cloths to wipe her face and offered the runners oxygen to help keep them going. As they rested on a lawn, Patty mentioned to Jim, "My foot's bothering me."

When they reached 190th Street in Redondo Beach, their first day's destination, they were huffing and straining. Their faces, arms, and legs were streaked with perspiration. Two motorcycle policemen fell in with them, their lights flashing. Patty and Jim were picking up speed, coming down the hill into the marina, when Patty remarked again, "Dad, my foot really hurts!"

"I think it's in your mind," answered Jim. "I can't do anything now. Let's wait until we stop and I'll look at it."

"There's Mom and Richard and Sam," Patty pointed. "They made it!"

"Look at that crowd!" beamed Jim. "Take my hand Patty, let's finish this together."

They dashed the final hundred yards, nearly airborne, their hands clenched together as they hit the red, white, and blue tape. They were swooped up into an electric current of excitement. Bulbs flashed. Questions popped at them. Redondo Beach Mayor David Hayward congratulated Jim and Patty and pinned Junior Fire Marshal Badges on their shirts.

"Stand a little closer so we can get your picture!" one reporter directed, maneuvering them into position.

The ceremonies were over almost as quickly as they started, and the family headed for the motor home. Jim and Patty wanted to shower and change before they were escorted to dinner.

"What's wrong?" Dotty asked, noticing Patty's limp.

"I can hardly walk on my foot. I think my shoes were too small."

Nine o'clock that evening, Dotty recorded her recollections and reflections of the day's events in her journal:

Miles run: 24.7. I decided to use red ink to describe this red letter day. The send-off from the B.P. mall was greater than any of us expected. Jim & Pat say that the motorcycle escort from town to town was exciting. Rich said he overheard two cyclists talking, and they said, "There must be someone important coming to hold traffic up in such a way."

We were escorted to dinner (all 5 of us; Rich is with us for tonight only). It was exquisite dining with a wonderful view of the beach, bike way and ocean. Our bus boy is a runner and very appreciative of Patty's attempt . . . he wanted a "T" shirt. I guess all runners are alike.

Everyone is asleep except guess who. I am sitting on the floor where the light is the best. I am going to call it a day as the alarm is set for 4:30.

Almost as an afterthought, Dotty added, "Pat's foot is hurting. We applied ice. It is the top of her foot."

13   *California: The Broken Journey*

"DADDY, my foot's killing me!"

"We can't stop now! You can usually push yourself, Patty. Can't you bear it a little longer?"

"I guess so." Patty looked away, pretending she was gazing at the ocean. Waves surging up to the breakwater shattered with a roar against the rocks. Sea gulls, screeching above them, wheeled out over the water.

Was this their second or third day? She couldn't remember. They were on the coastal highway and she breathed in the salty air as if it were anesthesia to deaden her pain. The pain enveloped her, consumed her. It throbbed rhythmically in her foot, streaked up her legs, charged through her body, slid down her arms, and poked at her wrists and fingers. It banged inside her head, a jangling pain that irritated all her nerves.

She was ashamed that she let it possess her that way. *I can't disappoint Daddy,* she thought. *I wish I could take my foot off and freeze it in the ocean until it deadens this awful pain; then I could run.*

She was falling farther and farther behind her father, struggling to make herself put her foot on the ground, fighting to forget the pain. But when her father was out of sight, she broke down and sobbed, burying her face in her shirt. Her entire body shook, and she couldn't stop herself from weeping; the tears rushed from her eyes and bathed her cheeks.

She sucked in the air and tried to bring herself out of it. *I can't let Daddy see me crying. I've got to stop this,* she chastised herself. *I've got to block out the pain!*

When she glanced up, she saw her father waiting for her. She wiped her face to try to hide the tears, but the dirt from the road stained her cheeks and shirt.

Just as Patty reached Jim, a carload of boys squealed up beside them. A couple of guys stretched out the windows and started slinging frozen fish at Patty and Jim.

"Youuww!" Jim yelped and jumped; one fish had struck his foot. Fortunately, the fish skimmed by Patty, missing her. The car spun off, the boys laughing raucously.

"Is it a bird? Is it a plane? No! It's super fish!" Patty joked, attempting a cheery front.

Jim saw that she'd been crying, but he teased her back, trying to keep her mind off her foot.

The fourth day they reached Port Hueneme, and Patty and Jim had completed 87.6 miles. But the pain in Patty's foot plagued her incessantly, and soaking it, wrapping it, and taking aspirin provided no relief. That morning her foot was more swollen that it had ever been, and she couldn't stand on it. Jim and Dotty had to carry her to the bathroom and back to her bunk.

Dotty looked at Jim and urged, "Let's take Patty to the hospital and have her foot x-rayed."

It was a sleepy seven o'clock when the nurse phoned for the emergency doctor. After he arrived and examined Patty's foot, x-rays were taken and read. "I'll have to consult an orthopedic specialist before I'll know the final results," the doctor said, "but I'm positive that her foot has a fracture and should be put in a cast for at least six weeks."

Jim retreated into himself. His daughter was sitting on the table and here were the x-rays displayed before him. The doctor and the nurse and Jim and Dotty were staring at each other. Jim realized that the trip might be over. *How do we go back? How can we go home and face our family? What will we tell our friends and Bob Bradach and John Baker in Oregon and the television and the newspapers? We've lined all this up. Not only is this trip over, but it's the finish of what I've tried so hard*

*to build up. Patty and I wanted to run across the United States. It's our
ultimate dream. Now it's our nightmare.*

Jim finally broke the silence. "We can't cast Patty's foot. She's
running one thousand miles to Portland." He then went on to
explain why they were running, how much publicity there had been,
and how disappointing it would be if they had to quit.

"This young lady won't do any more running," stated the doctor.
When she walks out of this hospital it will be with a cast on!"

"Before you do anything," answered Jim, "we'll go back to the
motor home and discuss what our plans are going to be. Would you
show us how to wrap her foot?"

"No, I won't!" the doctor replied crisply. "There's the matter of
liability!" But when he realized they were going to leave without
having Patty's foot put in a cast, he agreed to show Jim how to wrap
his own foot, so that he would know how to wrap his daughter's. He
also gave Patty a prescription for pain pills.

After Dotty wrapped Patty's foot the way the doctor showed Jim,
they ran 2.8 miles. Ten minutes before noon, Dotty called the doctor
for the diagnosis. It was definite: Patty had a stress fracture in the
third metatarsal bone of her left foot.

Back in the motor home, Jim joked about it at first, but soon
became quiet. They all knew how serious it was. He telephoned Bob
Bradach, who contacted a doctor who works with Olympic athletes.
He, too, recommended that Patty's foot be put in a cast.

By now Dotty was convinced. "Jim, let's quit and go home. If we
let Patty run, her foot could be permanently injured. It's not worth
it!"

Jim looked grimly at Patty. "You've heard what three doctors
think. Your mother wants us to stop. But a lot of people out there
are counting on you, Patty. They'll be disappointed if you quit, and
we've worked so hard to see this dream come true. It's up to you
to decide if you want to go on or stop." Jim forced a smile. "But just
remember. If you quit, I'll never speak to you again!" When he saw
Dotty's horrified expression, he chuckled. "I'm only kidding! Come
on; everyone looks so glum!"

"I know how much you want me to go on," Patty answered. "I

really want to help make your dream possible . . ." she paused to reflect. "I guess I'm just as greedy for it!"

The decision was made; they would go on. Dotty packed Patty's foot in ice; then Jim wrapped it. That afternoon they finished 12.7 miles to reach the 100.3-mile mark.

From that day on it became a challenge to Patty to make it on her broken foot. She read her Possibility Thinkers medallion and repeated the creed over and over to herself.

Jim gave pep talks to keep her motivated. "Life is like running the hurdles. When an athlete comes to a hurdle, he can go over it, around it, or through it. Life is made up of these hurdles, Patty. They're constantly before us. How we face them is important. Do we face them, or do we turn around and go back?

"Remember what Dr. Schuller said about climbing to the top of a mountain? This run is a mountain. There's nothing in the world that can stop us from reaching the peak, except one thing, maybe two. Do you know what that is?"

"If we were hit by a car?"

"That's one. If God strikes us down that's another. If I'm hit by a car and severely injured or killed, I want you to agree to go on. I want you to keep going without me and complete our dream and finish this run!"

"But, Daddy, I can't run without you!"

"I want you to, Patty. I may have to go back to work if we don't get enough miles in, and if I do I want you to promise to finish this. It will be our pact. Nothing will stop you from reaching that mountain peak."

At every rest break, Dotty soaked Patty's foot and drained a score of blisters with a hypodermic needle. Then Jim re-wrapped her foot. Because of the extra bulk, she had to wear a larger shoe.

At this point in the run, Patty's broken foot hadn't been confirmed publicly and news reports spoke tenderly about Patty's injury. One article stated:

Each of the 30,000 times a day her feet pound down on the pavement (the number needed to make 35 miles a day), it hurts. Both her ankles and insteps are taped and she is wearing knee braces, because there is added strain on the knees. The balls of her feet are so swollen that her toes don't touch the pavement when she rests her foot down.

Patty must have been listening . . . to Pete Strudwick, La Palma's footless runner, who says running is ninety percent mental and ten percent physical. Patty is running on one hundred percent heart.*

June 22, the city of Santa Barbara had a simple welcoming ceremony in front of City Hall. Officials from the Recreation and Parks Department presented Patty and Jim with pins imprinted with the City Seal. Television cameras recorded the event, which was later aired on the evening news.

Everywhere Dotty and Sam went, the cab-length signs on the motor home advertising Patty's run attracted crowds. In the ancient Spanish village of Guadalupe, the people in the market flocked about them. They were excited, wanting to know when the runners would arrive. They showed Dotty a copy of the Santa Maria paper that told about reporters who had searched for Jim and Patty but hadn't found them on the road. When Patty and Jim did arrive, there were the usual picture-taking sessions, in front of a Mexican cafe.

Pete Strudwick's arrival surprised them. He and his family were on their vacation, and he decided to intercept the Wilsons and run a few miles with them. It boosted Patty's and Jim's spirits immeasurably. Watching Pete run without feet always inspired Patty; now that her foot was broken, it meant that much more. It steeled her determination.

Bob Bradach brought Richard to be with the Wilsons over the weekend. Richard was distressed by the condition of his sister's feet.

"I don't know how she does it," he told his mother. "her foot looks awful! It's so swollen and covered with sores. I couldn't run on a foot like that!"

The tape Jim had been using had torn her skin off, leaving raw patches. It wasn't until later that Jim discovered he could attach the tape to the elastic bandage instead of her skin. Richard gave all of his time to Patty, helping her walk, watching over her when she ran.

*This article from the Wilsons' scrapbooks is not dated or identified.

Bob arranged for a massage and mineral bath for her, which helped Patty greatly. By Sunday they reached the 250.4 mile mark.

After it was announced that Patty's foot had been broken, the press continued to be sympathetic and Tom Ruppel wrote:

> The drugs for epilepsy slow her down some, as does the broken bone in her foot, but Patty Wilson will not stop running. Her long, blonde hair streams behind her as she and her father, Jim, puff up the long grades of Highway One.
>
> "There are too many people that believe in me," says Patty. "I can't quit."
>
> After a day's running from San Luis Obispo to Harmony, the sun-tanned . . . teenager relaxed in a Morro Bay laundromat, sitting on a washing machine, dangling her legs.
>
> Her feet were swollen and white. They were covered with raw sores where blisters had torn away.
>
> "People look at me and I represent several things," Patty explained. She wants to prove women can run long distances as well as men and that [people with epilepsy] are not persons to be locked away and forgotten.
>
> "I don't want a big sympathy story, she [added].*

By the end of June they were behind schedule and Patty was worried that Jim might have to return to work before they reached Portland. She was so panicked she started pushing herself to get the miles in. At San Simeon she paused briefly to look at the castle through binoculars, then she was off and running. When their break was over she was out before Jim, and she was running so well he often was unable to catch up to her.

People became Patty's motivation. She liked it when they ran with Jim and her, and enjoyed hearing the stories others shared about their lives.

A mountain of a man of Mexican descent dashed across both lanes of highway, dodging traffic to get to them. In his fifties, the man towered above Jim's six-foot frame. He asked Patty and Jim if he could take their picture, then he told them about himself.

"I had epilepsy when I was a young boy. I had it so bad I bit

*Tom Ruppel, *Morro Bay Sun-Bulletin,* June 1977.

through my lip. You can still see the scars," the man touched his bottom lip to show them. "I fell through a plate glass window. I had seizures like that at such a regular rate, I was confused. I feared I might kill myself."

His eyes brimmed with tears, and he paused a moment to regain his composure. "I want you to know how proud and humbled I am to meet you," he smiled at Patty. "You have so much courage to do this! I finally outgrew my epilepsy and I've worked for twenty-three years on a military base. I'll say prayers for you and so will my family. God bless you!" he waved them on.

June 30, Bob Bradach informed the Wilsons that they had miscalculated the mileage. According to the maps, the direct route up the center of California would have been just under one thousand miles to Portland. They knew the cooler coastal route would add a few more miles, but they never imagined that it would be an extra 250 to 350 miles. They were now on a thirteen-hundred-mile run. Jim and Dotty weren't sure they could obtain time off from work to finish the trip—their daily mileage had already been cut down because of Patty's injury.

"We plan to get up at four to get more miles in," Dotty noted at the bottom of that day's log.

The Wilsons didn't realize they were being tracked by CB radio fans, city police, Highway Patrol, and sheriffs, until people started telling them they had located them through one of these radio networks. The CBers and police always seemed to know where Patty and Jim stopped for a break, for how long, and how well Patty was faring on her foot. It was like being under CIA surveillance; Jim believed they knew when Patty and he went to the bathroom, if they scratched, frowned, or smiled.

Patty was entirely depleted after a steady thirty-mile day. She was in bed before sundown and out before dawn, but her early bedtime was becoming later and later because of visitors who wanted to meet her. Dotty and Sam were equally exhausted, playing hostess while trying to shepherd a flock of unruly details and never-ending difficulties. Once a water tank leaked, flooding the floor. Dotty had to make numerous daily phone calls to coordinate the run and arrange for special appearances. Then there were their usual routines, and Sam and she couldn't miss their daily mile or more of running. Only Jim could easily pull out that extra energy from his reserves to talk with people.

Despite their fatigue, the Wilsons enjoyed conversing with people. They were also pleased that the press was giving Patty's epilepsy such positive coverage. The run was accomplishing what they had hoped, which was to talk about epilepsy on a grass-roots level, to people from all phases of life, from the poorest to the wealthiest. The word *epilepsy* reverberated and echoed wherever they were. They heard people whispering or speaking loudly and unembarrassed about the "little girl with epilepsy." Or they exclaimed, "There's the epilepsy girl!"

Fortunately, Patty was strong enough to handle people's reactions. If she hadn't been, it might have broken her. When people asked Patty about her epilepsy, she brushed it off with such nonchalance she evaporated people's fears and prejudices. Her condition was no more serious to her than having a freckle on her nose. The majority responded with a positive warmth, but if Patty noticed that someone was put off or uneasy her attitude was, "That's their problem!"

There were times when the family felt the invasion of their privacy went too far: On July fifth, when they crossed San Francisco's Golden Gate Bridge, two television crews traced Patty to an outhouse, stood outside the door, and tried to interview her.

By the twentieth day, July 7, they'd achieved 605.3 miles. People were conserving water in California because of the drought, and even the laundromats were closed in some places. But the manager of the trailer park the Wilsons stayed at in Bodega Bay had seen the front page pictures of Patty crossing the Golden Gate. She was so overcome by the fact that Patty would be staying in her park, she turned on the water so Patty could take a shower. "I don't care if I do get in trouble for breaking the law," she told Dotty.

That same evening Patty became sick and starting throwing up.

She vomited so violently and for so long that Dotty was afraid she'd tear her insides apart if she continued.

The following morning Dotty wrote in her journal,

Today has started off rather poorly. It is noon now and Jim and Pat have only managed 3.8 miles. Pat was sick last night and . . . she did not get to bed until eleven thirty. This morning when we got back to where we had left off she began vomiting again. Finally at seven thirty they were able to start on the trail. She had to rest before she even completed a mile. It took several rest periods before she . . . said she had to have rest and we decided to break for a few hours. Patty felt much better when she was awakened. We decided to have some lunch and return to running.

When Jim and Patty resumed running, Dotty and Sam toured Fort Ross. The headwinds were so strong their baseball caps blew off their heads and they were whipped to and fro like rag dolls. Drivers struggled to keep their cars in the right lanes. It was beautiful, fierce, windswept country. Mountains stood in the sea. The etched-out road resembled a trail, and in places running room was a single shoe width. Patty and Jim gave up after five miles.

Saturday, July 9, headwinds continued at what seemed hurricane force. Patty still wasn't well; she was persecuted by diarrhea, which attacked her at unexpected and inopportune moments. The previous day they'd only completed nineteen miles and Jim was pressing to make up for the mileage. They were scheduled for a welcoming ceremony on Sunday at Fort Bragg, which was still about eighty-three miles away.

Sunday, when they realized they weren't going to make it to the ceremonies by three o'clock, they stopped. Dotty drove for just under eight miles, then dropped off Patty and Jim about two miles from town so they could come in running. For the ceremonies at the city's entrance, Patty stood in front of a gigantic slice from a red-wood tree, with a sign announcing: "Fort Bragg 1857." Patty received a silver charm in the shape of this gigantic tree, and was also given a live redwood tree as a symbol of long life and strength.

No matter how sick Patty had been or how much pain or fatigue she experienced, she was always smiling her radiant smile that warmed and charmed people everywhere she went. She couldn't conceal how incredibly tired and numb she felt or how sick she was. Her hazel eyes betrayed her, reflecting her agony.

A high school track team had come out to run four and a half miles with Patty into the campground. Since Patty was still so sick, she had decided not to attempt it. But when she saw how enthusiastic the team was she couldn't disappoint them, so she ran it with them. It had been an incredible two days for Patty. She had clocked in 39.3 miles Saturday and 36.6 on Sunday, fighting headwinds, weathering a bout of vomiting and diarrhea, and continual pain in her foot and knees.

On June 11 the Wilsons were up at five so they could cover the 7.7-mile stretch they had skipped in order to get to the Fort Bragg ceremonies. Before they began running, Patty called KPAM radio in Portland to give them an update on her progress, which the station reported daily.

When she started out, she ran about two steps and fell face down in the dirt, turning her ankle. She picked herself up, brushed herself off and started again. But at the 0.2-mile mark, when Dotty passed them in the R.V., Patty waved her down for a pit stop. Jim was upset that they were getting such a poor start, and he kept saying, "Lord, give me patience!"

During the previous two weeks Jim and Dotty had been trying frantically to obtain extra days off from work; now clearance had finally come through for both of them. They were free to finish the entire trip. Patty, more than anyone, was relieved that Jim could finish with her. Just the thought that he wouldn't be with her terrified her. She felt she couldn't make it alone or with anyone else.

Ordinarily Patty and Jim developed callouses, corns, and blisters on friction points of their feet and toes. To keep from chafing under their arms, inside their legs, and any other place where the motion of their stride could rub them raw, they lathered themselves with petroleum jelly every morning. Because Patty overcompensated for her broken foot, her step was off center and she developed an enormous, undrainable blister under the nail of her big toe, which added terribly to her discomfort.

Taping Patty's feet in the morning was an ordeal. After she

dressed and brushed her teeth she seemed to be awake, but when Jim started to wrap her foot she'd fall asleep. Her foot couldn't be relaxed; she had to hold it in the right position before they could tape it. Jim and Dotty yelled at Patty, and nudged her or threw wet wash cloths at her to keep her alert.

Patty looked like a mummy with her knees, parts of her leg, and feet heavily wrapped and bandaged. Her stride was so awkward it threw her body off balance. Patty turned her foot inward, bearing her weight on the outside of her foot, which wore down the outside of her left shoe completely. She had already worn out nine pairs of shoes. Only her steel mental fiber and gutsy determination, and her father's prodding, kept her going against her body's constant cry to quit.

A continuous stream of people sometimes refreshed, other times flooded Patty and Jim. Bicyclists from all over the United States and Canada assisted them, stopping to visit and advise Jim of the road conditions, steepness of grades, and the weather conditions. (Most bicyclists were riding south so the winds would propel them rather than oppose them. If Jim had consulted bicyclists before starting, he would have known that by starting in Portland and finishing in California they would not have to battle headwinds.)

One family drove all the way from Santa Rosa just to meet Patty and Jim, and they offered them food and cold drinks. A Girl Scout camp lined the road and cheered for her. Passing motorists honked and waved, or gave them the clenched fist or thumbs-up salute. But there were those drivers who deliberately tried to pick Patty and Jim off by driving as close as possible without hitting them. Then there were a few who yelled, "Is that as fast as you can run? Run faster!"

July 17, Patty and Jim spotted a man with two children pulling his car over and parking directly across from them. He tucked one child under his arm, took the other by the hand, and dashed across the four-lane highway, which was swarming with traffic. Patty and Jim stopped, watching with horror and hoping the man and his children would not be struck down. When he reached them, he introduced himself and said, "I want to wish you well. Would you mind if I run a ways with you? I'll stay behind."

"Certainly! You can run all the way to Portland with us if you like," Jim enthused.

The man was so thrilled he left his children, about four and six years old, on the shoulder of the road and ran a few steps with Patty and Jim. Jim realized the man was handicapped. Then the man waved them on, satisfied to say he'd run with Patty, and scrambled back across the highway with his children.

Later that day Patty and Jim reached the redwoods, where Highway 101 knelt by the sea, and quickly ascended nine miles to twelve hundred feet. They were running at a relaxed pace through an aisle of stately trees. The redwoods were an ancient cathedral of majestic beauty and awesome height, adorned in a silver mist, with altars of graceful ferns and elegant rhododendrons. Birds darted in and out of pine-needled rafters beneath the ceiling of the sky. A hush fell across this forest sanctuary, as if a thousand-voice choir were poised to sing.

The wonder of it drew Patty and Jim into a reverent mood. Usually they made up silly stories about the scenery, now they were absorbed in a philosophical discussion.

"Why did God make hills?" Patty asked her father.

"God made hills so we can appreciate the downhills. Everytime we make it to the top of a hill, we're blessed with the luxury of going down."

But as the afternoon wore on, and they were creeping up the nine-mile grade, they began to doubt their theory that God had designed hills that went both up and down—this one seemed to go up and up forever. Upgrades required their entire energy and more. What irritated them most was they didn't receive credit for extra effort or mileage.

They leaned forward, breathing in, breathing out, their legs working harder, their arms pumping. They were marionettes and an invisible puppeteer was controlling their strings, first their right arms and left legs, then their left arms and right legs—pulling-pumping, pulling-pumping. Sweat coursed down their faces and bodies; they huffed and puffed, gasping for air to finish the last 2.3 miles of their nine-mile trek.

14 *Oregon: Magnificent Marathon*

TO CELEBRATE crossing the state line, the Brookings-Harbor High School cross-country team joined Patty and Jim the last ten miles. A crowd of well-wishers and television and radio crews had waited more than an hour to witness the event.

"Welcome to Oregon," greeted a huge wood marker. Patty rested on a log piling, gave out a sigh of exhaustion, then slapped her father's hand in a final "we made it" gesture.

"Sorry I took so long," she apologized. According to their original calculations they were not only more than an hour late, but a week overdue.

One sports editor covering the event noted Patty's habitual joking and bantering. She had a special name for the throngs of people who watched them run or came out to see her. ". . . Patty, who named them, always stops for the Lookeelous," Bill Dixon wrote. "In a way they are her creation. And they are coming out to see something no other woman has ever done before. . . . Monday at five P.M. she stretched the record to 953 miles when she crossed the border." The lengthy article concluded, "Patty ducks behind the camper when the interview's over. 'Lookeelous,' she says to Sam. They laugh."*

Newspaper readers were offended by the story and Patty was horrified. Her silly commentary on the landscape and people was never meant to insult anyone, it was just the way she and her father

*Bill Dixon, *Coos Bay World,* July 1977.

entertained themselves. Patty had taken "Lookeelou" from a California realtor's television ad in which a couple arrived unannounced to look at a home for sale. The wife remarked to her husband, "Lookee Lou!" The point of the ad was that the seller needed a realtor to save them from the "Lookee Lous."

Patty and Jim had been told that Oregon was the running state, and they anticipated having track teams with them to keep their morale boosted and help raise money for the Epilepsy Center in Oregon. The last thing they wanted to do was offend the public and fellow runners.

Time scurried by when they had runners with them, and Jim enjoyed amusing them with tales of past adventures. It filled him with pleasure to replay their more spectacular feats again and again, remembering each detail, his hands gesturing to emphasize a point, never breaking the rhythm of his stride.

Although Patty was less exuberant than her father, she was still animated and bubbly. She enjoyed talking about common concerns, school, the beach, favorite songs, friends, and her epilepsy, if someone asked her about it. But when Jim and she were alone she belted out songs, doing her Barbara Streisand imitation. But her theme song for her journey was "Looks Like We Made It," a song Barry Manilow had made popular.

The following morning the Brookings-Harbor team joined them again. Trotting along the highway, Patty and the team members chattered, laughed, and teased. Then suddenly there was a natural lull in the conversation. Only Rick, a boy from Brookings, and Patty continued talking.

"I have epilepsy, too," he said matter-of-factly.

Patty didn't think it was a strange or serious statement, but there was a long silent pause, as if the film broke, interrupting the most exciting moment in a movie.

"I never knew you had epilepsy!" one of his teammates finally exclaimed.

"I didn't either!" someone else added, shocked.

A roar of comments and questions flew at Rick.

"I never had the courage to tell anyone before!" he answered.

Patty realized what a risk it was for Rick to expose his epilepsy. He lived in a small town, not a metropolis like Orange County where he could bury his secret. Now it was out and would be talked about all over town. Patty understood it was a release for Rick to talk to someone else who had it. They discussed their common problems and medications they were taking. It was a moment Patty would always remember. One more Candle of Understanding had been lit and was burning bravely. She knew her pain, unendurable as it sometimes was, was somehow worth it.

Wednesday, July 20, their thirty-third day, they were in Gold Beach. John Baker had joined them sometime before in Crescent City, and was sleeping in a sleeping bag on the ground so he could travel with the Wilsons. John invited Sam to help him with public relations. They would drive ahead to make arrangements for special appearances, the track teams, the press, and television and radio.

The first day Sam and John started out, she had to set one thing straight. His cigarettes were sitting on the dashboard. Jim and Dotty didn't smoke and Sam didn't like it, so she announced, "I don't want you smoking around my sister. You should quit!"

John agreed to replace smoking with running. He challenged Sam to a contest: Who could run the most miles through Oregon, Sam or John? Sam tore up John's pack of cigarettes and threw them in the trash. They put in 18.9 miles that day, even though John was not a runner. He was sunburned, stiff, sore, and filthy from the road, but he stuck to his agreement.

Although Sam was two years younger than Patty, they were almost the same height and both had long blonde hair. Sam ordinarily ran a mile or two a day, then stayed in the background working with her mother. Now that she was out on the road, passersby mistook Sam for Patty. It infuriated Sam so much she put on a plain T-shirt that didn't advertise the run.

Ten and two-tenths miles north of Gold Beach, Patty and Jim reached one thousand miles. When Patty was first told she had to run three hundred extra miles, she was distraught and feared she would go crazy. She would wake in the morning and think, *Oh no, nine*

hundred more miles, instead of six hundred. I can't take it. I can't go on.
I'm in too much pain. I think I'd rather die than go on.

Jim advised her, "Don't think any farther than right now. Just take
it day by day."

That's a good idea, she thought. *I'll make my goal one day at a time.*
She had clung to that until they hit one thousand miles; then she felt
she'd crashed into a brick wall. They were out in the middle of
nowhere. Cows grazed disinterestedly in a nearby field. Dotty was
recording the mileage on her clipboard, and Patty and Jim held up
a one thousand mile sign so Dotty could capture the momentous
occasion with her camera.

Patty was smiling during the picture-taking session, but she was
thinking, *this should be the end of our trip. If this were the finish, there
would be a crowd here to greet us, and I would be through running. I have
to go all the way to Portland, but I've accomplished my part. This isn't fair!
I've done the job I agreed to do. Why can't we stop here? Daddy keeps telling
me why, but I still can't figure it out—over three hundred more miles! I can't
take the pain any longer. I'm so tired. I'll never make it!*

When they started out again, Patty was deeply disheartened. Her
depression lingered for several days, and she was beginning to wonder if she would ever come out of it, when the Bandon track club
came out and ran several days with her. This helped bring her out
of her despair and renew her spirits.

Throughout Oregon, back-to-back track teams pulled Patty along.
Whenever reporters interviewed her, one of her first requests was,
"If anybody wants to come run, we welcome anybody and every-
body."

Friday, July 22, Patty met the parents of Steve Prefontaine. Steve
had been Coos Bay's American distance record holder in six events
at the time of his death in 1975, in an automobile accident. Once
he had been voted most popular track athlete in the world.

Patty visited his grave, and when she knelt to place a single red
rose, she paused to read his headstone. "Our beloved son and
brother who raced through life now rests in peace." Patty was so
touched tears wet her eyes.

As a further tribute to Steve, she wore a "Pre's Trail Run" T-shirt out on the road. That evening the Wilsons had dinner with the Prefontaines, who showed them Steve's room and scrapbook. When Patty turned the last page she was surprised to see there were clippings about her pasted in the book. Everything had been a shrine to Steve; now here she was included in the pages of his book. She was overwhelmed to think his parents considered her so highly.

July 24, they were joined by runners from Florence, Oregon. Kelly Davis and Stan Goodell drove eighty miles to run with Patty. The same day Patty met Bill and Pat Gormallys who, were walking from monument to monument around the United States border. They had started in Providence, Rhode Island, in July of 1975 and walked eight thousand miles. It was interesting to meet other pioneer travelers.

Patty had been talking so much to reporters and other visitors that she could hardly speak. Her voice was hoarse. Fatigue, her incredible pain, the strain of stopping to give interviews was hampering their progress. They were five days from the finish and Patty was so anxious to have it over, she announced, "If anyone wants a story, they better put on their tennis shoes and come out and run with me, because I'm not going to wait!"

Sunday, July 24, Richard flew into Eugene to join his family, but he couldn't find them. At the police department he spoke to the desk clerk. "I'm trying to find my sister, Patty Wilson. Do you know where she is?"

"We can't help you unless an all-points bulletin has already been put out on her," the clerk replied, unaware that Patty wasn't lost, but running through his state. When Richard finally found his family in Florence, he was relieved and happy to be with them again. It had been a long, lonely thirty-seven days.

Originally, Patty would have been in Eugene at this point. The Wilsons had been told it was "Track City USA," but due to a mix-up in communications there was a sparse reception and no one turned out to run with them on Steve Prefontaine's trail.

"We're a little bitter because we were looking toward Eugene as a highlight," Jim told a reporter. "These smaller cities opened up their doors and hearts. It wasn't that we were looking for freebies

—we just thought the word 'run' was synonymous with Eugene."

"It was a total waste of time, going into Eugene, so we cut it off," John added.

Although their statements angered the city, Patty was silently relieved; their change in routing cut out seventeen extra miles.

On Monday just south of Corvallis, they met an executive who had never told anyone except his wife that he had epilepsy. If he ever revealed it, he said, he knew he wouldn't be able to secure employment, and he would risk losing his present position. But when he read that Patty was coming through Corvallis, he asked the director of a local radio station if he would do a public information interview with him about Patty's run and epilepsy. When the interview was aired, this executive talked about epilepsy, announcing that he, too, had it. Then he asked the radio audience to support Patty's efforts.

When he met Patty, he told her, "I'm proud of you! I know what you're doing will do some good." She was surprised at how relieved the man seemed, as if he'd been accused of committing a felony years before. Now that he'd turned himself in and received his pardon, he was free!

Later, a young girl asked Patty, "Will you let me run with you? I used to run track, but now I have diabetes and they won't let me anymore."

"Sure!" Patty grinned. "You can run as far as you want with us. Come on," she waved. The girl scampered only a few yards with them because she was wearing sandals, but she seemed thrilled she could go even a short way with Patty. Later an elderly woman in her eighties, nearly blind and deaf, stopped Patty on the highway.

"You're doing a wonderful thing. You're so sweet." She cupped Patty's face between her crinkled hands, then embraced her and cradled her back and forth, weeping. Patty was so touched, she cried with her.

Wednesday, July 27, Patty and Jim met Governor Bob Straub on the steps of the capitol in Salem. He, too, was a running enthusiast who put in two miles every morning.

"I promise to run the last mile with you," he told Patty. "You won't run too fast for me, will you?"

"No," Patty shook her head and grinned shyly.

"We're helping to keep your beautiful state clean," chirped Jim, holding up a half-dozen bottles he'd found. "We pick up bottles to make money, but we haven't made much. Bottles along the roadside here are scarce!"

Governor Straub then invited the Wilson family to his office, where he gave Patty a book—a photographic essay of Oregon—and a pen he gave away at bill signings.

Thursday, one journalist recognized Patty's ability to greet people warmly. At the same time, she captured a glimpse of the incredible way Patty masked her emotions and hid her enemy, pain.

> As she neared Canby—she still had time to wave to a passing train conductor, acknowledge honking horns . . . and accept a bouquet. . . .
>
> She may be late, though. It's people like Charlie Bushman . . . who slow her down. But she doesn't really care and she was all smiles when he presented her with a bouquet of roses and carnations when she stopped for a drink of water.
>
> "I met her out near Woodburn this morning," said Bushman, "and I followed her on the way. She's just great. She's doing something I never could do. I'm heavy, I have arthritis and I was born with club feet."
>
> When she pauses for a rest and has a few moments alone, the smile fades, the brow wrinkles and she massages her foot. The pain is with her always. The drugs she takes to inhibit the seizures are depressants she must battle every step of the thirty-one miles a day.
>
> But the shoe goes back on, her braces flash in the sunlight as she smiles at her family and new friends, and, with hardly a limp, she steps back on the side of the highway to finish her long journey.*

Patty revealed only what she wanted people to know about herself and allowed them to see only what she wanted them to see. A very private person, she never would get used to people probing her, questioning her. She was willing to volunteer certain information, like telling them her foot hurt, but she never revealed the extreme extent of her pain.

That evening, when they were eating supper, Mike Weiss of the

*Connie Hofferber, *The* [Portland] *Oregonian,* 29 July 1977.

Oregon Journal asked Patty and Jim about their future plans after their finale the following day.

"I'd like to get some sleep," answered Patty. "I need to give my body a rest."

"What do you think about your daughter, Mr. Wilson?"

Jim grinned proudly and said, "She'll 'try something bigger' next year. I have a vision and it might sound corny, but I'd like to make her kind of like an Elvis or Cher. They'd say *Patty* and know who it is."

Friday, July 29, 1977. Patty was lying on her bunk listening to music, waiting to start the last sixteen miles. She pulled in her breath, then sighed deeply, emptying her lungs. She couldn't believe it would all be over in a few hours. She could hear the clamour outside, reporters were already waiting to talk to her. She was trapped in her thoughts, reminiscing about what had brought her this far and what was supposed to take her on. She wasn't sure how, but she had to finish these last few miles.

She sat up and her head began to swim. The dizziness that had plagued her throughout her trip had returned. She was incredibly tired; she hadn't slept well because her foot ached so much. Her mind kept telling her this was supposed to be a magnificent, important occasion, but she wasn't convinced.

She laid her head down again, half closing her eyes. She heard her theme song coming. She'd listened to it again and again until she knew it by memory. When Barry Manilow began to sing, it was her escape. Patty allowed herself to slip into the mood of the song. She wrapped the words around her, remembering her deep depression. Her thoughts slid away. Then she heard her favorite refrain. "Looks Like We Made It" sounded beautiful to her, and she lifted her spirit up with it.

She sang to herself quietly, changing the lyrics to fit her own definition, making them her own. So many times on their journey she thought she'd go crazy, crazy from her pain. She couldn't let her father down and she couldn't go on without him. She was drowning in her darker feelings, but then the song unexpectedly pulled her to shore, rescuing her as it had so many times before. She was gaining strength, renewing her will to go on. She was going to make it!

"Come on, Patty, let's get going," her father said, motioning, breaking her mood. "Looks Like We Made It" echoed once more and faded.

She stood and tried to shake off the dizziness, but she was outside before she knew it, engulfed again. The chaos of reporters, spectators, and traffic picked her up and carried her down a raging river, through white, swirling waters. After six miles, Patty and Jim took a break before their last ten miles, but there was no rest for Patty. Questions were thrust at her like swords.

"How'd you get the idea for the run?"

"It wasn't my idea. It was Dad's idea, his dream, his brain child."

"How do you feel about breaking your long-distance record?"

"I feel great about what I've done, but people around me think it's a bigger deal than I do."

Runners joined them, swelling their ranks. Patty stayed in the middle of the pack, never changing her slow steady pace. Reporters stayed with her, continuing to note her observations.

"I'm so dizzy," remarked Patty. "I get very high and very low during these long runs." Her statement was recorded.

"Somebody back there was taking a picture of my feet!" she snapped irritably. "I don't see why they would want a picture of my shoes. If they're trying to take a picture of my foot, there's no way they can photograph all this pain!"

Governor Straub was there for the last mile as he had promised, wearing a billed cap. His six-feet, four-inch frame dwarfed Patty. Except for her muscled legs, she was petite, and fifteen pounds lighter than she was when she started.

Television camera crews were following them now, but Patty was lost in the congestion. Children in black and gold track suits surrounded Patty and Governor Straub, and they were tripping over them.

"Stay back! Stay out of the way," the Governor urged, trying to motion them back, but it was useless.

As they neared City Hall, they could hear the clocks chiming noon and see the enormous crowd which was being filled with more people on their lunch hour. On the porch, a paper sign was taped across huge concrete pillars. "Welcome Patty," it greeted.

Jim broke into a wide grin; it thrilled him to see everyone cheering for his daughter. He glanced over to see if Patty were smiling, but she wasn't. She looked so weary it sobered him. For an instant he wondered, *What kind of a father am I to make her run on an injured foot? She cried and cried night after night with the pain.* His guilt overcame him and he shuddered, but the yelling and whistling and tumultous applause cut off his moment of regret. Jim loved to watch the people straining to see Patty. "Where's is she? Is that Patty?"

Patty couldn't get over it; people seemed to be everywhere. She felt she would suffocate as the mob knotted itself more tightly around her.

"Where's Patty? Where's Patty?" Connie McCready, representative for Portland's Mayor, kept asking.

Patty was thrust through the mob of people like an infant being born. Jim was pushed into the background as if he had no part in this birth, but he didn't care. This was his daughter's hour of glory.

People shoved each other, jockeying to get close to Patty. It scared her; everytime she moved to give herself room, people pressed in on her. She started to panic!

"I'm having a little trouble breathing," she finally managed to say in one of the numerous microphones pointing at her face.

People backed away so quickly, Patty realized they were afraid she might have a seizure. She didn't care what they feared; she had all the space she needed and she could breathe.

When the cacophony finally fell to a low murmur, Connie McCready gave Patty a medal from the Mayor's office, then told her, "You have a quality I admire. Anybody who can run so well and can go so far ought to be in politics. You're the best example of 'people power' I have seen in a long, long time."

When she kissed Patty, the cries and applause went up. After the crowd finally quieted some, Patty was asked to say something. When she spoke her voice was still hoarse and she appeared extremely exhausted.

"I'm glad it's over. I feel great about what I've done. The end is super!" she beamed. "It was that long stretch in between Orange County and Portland that was so tough. *Oh, but the people! They helped me make it!"*

Governor Straub took her right hand and raised it into the air and proclaimed, "Today is 'Patty Wilson Day' in Oregon."

The crowd roared. There was a great surge of emotion. People were wiping tears from their eyes, trying to refrain from crying. Others wept openly. The brief ceremonies were over but the milling crowd lingered. Those who stayed to shake Patty's hand—or to touch her—didn't know what to say.

There were the usual picture sessions. One photographer requested a picture of Patty and the Governor together and then asked, "Mr. Governor, would you move away? We'd like a picture of Patty." Patty thought this was funny and she giggled to herself.

But there had been a terrible comedy of errors going on during the ceremonies. Dotty missed them entirely because she couldn't find a place to park the RV, nor could she squeeze her way through the crowd when she finally did find a spot. Then limousines were waiting to whisk Patty and her family to a luncheon in her honor, but Sam was somehow left standing on the steps of City Hall. The Wilsons thought she was with Richard and Richard thought she was with them. Sam was delivered two hours later, in tears, to the Wilson's hotel room.

That afternoon Dr. Howard Geist, an orthopedist, examined Patty's foot and said, "Yes, it's definite; it's unquestionable." X-rays verified that Patty had suffered a stress fracture her first day out. Despite her fatigue, Dr. Geist added, she was in fine physical condition and wasn't "any worse than a lot of people after a game of golf." He advised Patty not to do any forced running and assured Dotty that she had passed the point of any complications from the fracture.

Her broken foot had overshadowed the one serious problem they had feared might occur. Despite the stress of her journey and her extreme pain, she hadn't had a seizure.

The final statistics showed that Patty had run 1,310.5 miles. She had done the equivalent of fifty marathons in forty-two consecutive days, and averaged thirty-one miles a day. She had worn out fifteen pairs of shoes. They had collected $15.67 in bottles and $4.91 in coins; and Sam won her bet with John Baker, completing 102.5 to his 100.4 miles.

The second day after the finale, Jim, Dotty, and Richard returned to California. Patty and Sam stayed in Portland with John Baker's family. A couple days later in the evening, Patty felt like something was wrong with her, but she blamed it on fatigue. Her left leg kept twitching while she was watching television. When she started to tremble, she figured she really needed rest, so she went to bed and fell right to sleep.

Patty and Sam were sleeping together, and Sam had barely fallen into a light slumber when she was startled awake. As she turned over, she saw that Patty's arms and legs were tangled in her blankets. Patty's entire body was convulsing uncontrollably.

Sam scrambled out of bed and shouted, "John! Come here! Something's wrong with Patty!"

By the time John and Sam returned to the bedroom, Patty's convulsion was over. She'd rolled herself up in her blankets, and she was sleeping soundly, as if nothing had happened. John knew Patty would be all right, but he moved her against the wall to prevent her from falling out of bed if she should have another seizure. Later Patty remembered her leg had twitched while she was watching television, but she had no recollection of her convulsion.

15 *Welcome Home, Patty*

ON AUGUST 13, a welcome home reception was held for Patty in Buena Park. She opened the ceremonies by lighting a large white Candle of Understanding on the stage in the community center. She was rested and relaxed and tanned, as if she'd been on an extended vacation. It was difficult to believe she was the same girl who had run 1,310 miles on a broken foot, her face drawn by exhaustion and pain. Instead of her usual ponytail and her uniform of shorts and T-shirt, she was dressed in a skirt and knit blouse. Her honey blonde hair hung freely and gracefully to her waist.

That evening Patty was presented with trophies, plaques, and flowers to commend her for breaking her long distance record and for carrying the light for epilepsy. Bob Bradach had made an enormous collage of 1,310 pennies in the shape of a girl runner. The California Epilepsy Society gave Patty airline tickets to attend a conference on epilepsy in Washington, D.C. State Assemblyman Chet Wray proclaimed August 13 "Patty Wilson Day" in California.

A few weeks later, Patty was thrilled to work with Henry Winkler of *Happy Days'* fame. Henry, then EFA's Honorary Youth Chairman, and Patty filmed a public service television spot together for a national campaign to help educate the public and to promote a positive image for epilepsy.

At the end of August Dotty, Patty, and Sam flew to Washington, D.C. to attend the EFA's national conference. For Patty, the highlight was participating in the newly formed Epilepsy Youth Association (EYA) meetings. It was here that she met John Loftus, a congenial, six-foot plus pre-med student and president of EYA.

In his address to youth at the conference John challenged, "The EYA hopes to become one of the most active and strongest supporting branches of the EFA in our attempt to promote the human rights of the two million persons with epilepsy. If we involve youth, and educate them before they develop misconceptions and prejudices about epilepsy, some of the social problems could be drastically reduced."

"I'm really excited about the goals of the EYA," Patty told John. "Next year Dad and I are planning a two thousand mile run to St. Louis. I'd like to raise a lot of money for research and help local chapters like ours. Why don't you come along with us on our next run and help us out?" Patty teasingly returned John's challenge.

At the conference Patty learned for the first time about her own seizures. She discovered that *the epilepsies* is a more accurate term than *epilepsy,* because it covers a number of disorders of the nervous system, centered in the brain. This made sense to Patty, considering the several different types of seizures she had experienced.

She found out epilepsy is a democratic disorder. It happens to people of all ages, and can strike at any time or any stage of life, from infancy to old age. It has no regard for social or economic status. It doesn't care about race, religion, or place of origin. Some one hundred thousand Americans and their families discover this fact every year, because it happens to them.

Patty also learned that the terminology used to describe *the epilepsies* had been internationalized. The convulsions she had in third and sixth grades were now called *generalized tonic-clonic,* instead of *grand mal.* Patty knew that this type lasted only a few minutes. She would lose consciousness and fall to the floor, and then most or all of her body flailed convulsively. Some people at the conference told Patty that they had broken their teeth or cut their mouths because someone had put a spoon or pencil between their teeth, supposedly to keep them from swallowing their tongues. This was one of the strange and persistant myths that baffled Patty.

She was grateful no one had ever tried to wedge something in her mouth. Despite their hysteria, the teachers had handled her convulsion properly. Her sixth grade teacher had tied a ribbon in her hair and turned her on her side so that she wouldn't choke on her saliva, and moved her to a safe place where she could rest when it was over.

Patty had also had *absences,* —formerly called *petit mal*—seizures, which were momentary lapses of consciousness from five to twenty seconds. Patty now realized she was probably having absences seizures when her teachers were upset with her for not listening or missing a set of instructions.

Most confusing to her had been the *complex partial (psychomotor)* seizures, like her first one in seventh grade when she was sitting in the bean bag, or the others when she was running with her father and during cross-country races. This is the most complicated type and can be manifested several ways. Chewing and lip smacking, staring and confusion, abdominal pains and headaches are only a few of the symptoms. Changes in color perception, spots before the eyes, buzzing and ringing in the ears, or dizziness can also occur. Sometimes complex partial seizures are marked by fear, rage, or anger.

Like Patty's, the seizure may last from a minute to several hours, and is sometimes followed by long hours of deep sleep. Usually there is no memory of any event that went on during that period. Patty was also discovering that no two people had the same types of seizures, and that epilepsy is still a complicated, mysterious disorder.

At the EFA conference, Patty had also been warned about some of the harsher realities of having epilepsy. In November, when she turned sixteen, she faced one for the first time. She went to apply for her driver's permit. When she read the question on the application that asked "Do you have lapses of consciousness?" her hand started to shake. She thought to herself, *I'll be so disappointed if I don't get my permit. All my friends are driving. What if I put "No" in here?* she wondered, struggling with the question. *But no, I can't lie! Every paper in Orange County told the world that I have epilepsy.*

"You'll have to have your doctor's clearance first," the examiner explained to Patty when she handed him her application. "After you've seen your doctor and he returns the papers, then your application will go before a state review board. If it's been less than a year since your last seizure your application will be denied."

"How long will it be before I know if I get my license or not?" Patty asked.

"Two or three months," he replied, "but you can take your writ-

ten test now. Once you pass it we can start processing the paper-
work." The man stamped her papers and handed Patty her test.

"Thanks." Patty half smiled, and tried to act nonchalant. She
didn't want him to know that her heart was racing and she would
have cried, but she couldn't let herself. Although people at the
conference had told her what it was like to apply for a job or a
driver's license, she hadn't expected it to be so hard.

When she was standing at the desk trying to concentrate on the
questions, the reality of her situation struck her with cold force:
They're not going to change everything just because I ran 1,310 miles!
They're not going to say to me, "Well, in your case we can let you drive, let
you have a job, and give you life insurance at a fair rate because you've
proven that people with epilepsy are normal. You've made and broken long
distance running records, so we'll make an exception." The unfairness of
it staggered her.

Patty's application was turned down, but Jim and Dotty appealed
it. Six months later Patty appeared before a judge.

"This is awful!" she whispered to her father in court. "They've
lumped me in with the alcoholics, drunk drivers, and drug abusers!"

When the Wilsons' lawyer made his appeal before the judge, he
mentioned Patty's 1,310 mile run. The judge interrupted their lawyer and surprised them all when he told Patty, "I've been reading
about you in the newspapers and I read your story in our Sunday
magazine, *Family Weekly."* After a brief, warm discussion with Patty,
he rapped his gavel. "License granted!"

Throughout the year, Patty had received accolades from several
organizations. She was honored with the Young American Award
by the Explorer Scouts. *Reader's Digest* published her story and gave
her a Service Award. She received the Outstanding Athlete Award
from the Los Angeles Police Athletic and Running Club, and the
First Annual John Baker Award from Brigham Young University.

In the meantime, the EFA took over Jim's planning of the two
thousand mile run. They decided the "Super Run" would start at
Minneapolis, Minnesota and conclude in Washington, D.C. Jim and
Patty would go through more major cities across the Midwest and
Northeast than if they were to cross the vast desert and sparsely

populated communities that lay between California and St. Louis.

John Loftus became so enthusiastic about the Super Run he accepted Patty's invitation. He would travel with the Wilsons as liaison and coordinator.

The theme chosen for the "Patty Wilson Super Run" was "2,000 miles—for $2,000,000—to help 2,000,000 people with epilepsy." It was originally scheduled to start in June when school was out, but due to the intricacies of planning a trip of this magnitude, the starting date was moved to the fifth of August.

When the EFA approached Allstate Life Insurance Company about giving a leave of absence to Jim, Allstate agreed not only to give Jim the time off, but offered to underwrite all expenses for the Super Run, which were estimated at $200,000. Jim would receive his regular agent's salary and their expenses on the trip were covered, but Jim and Patty would not receive anything more. All monies she raised were to go directly to epilepsy.

"I want to make the Super Run," Patty told her father, "and help the cause of epilepsy, but I can't stand the pressure. Every time I think about it I feel like the success or failure of the run relies on me. In my mind the Super Run is Patty Wilson and Patty Wilson is the Super Run. That's awesome; I can't stand it! I've been having dreams about it and I don't like my dreams anymore."

Like most dreams, Patty's were mixed up. Patty dreamed she was visiting a famous movie star in Las Vegas. The star had written Patty a letter telling her, "Keep it going, Patty!" Then Patty saw herself in the audience watching this star perform. Her fans were there applauding for her, screaming for her when she finished a song. Suddenly Patty was alone with the star.

"Your family's gone!" someone interrupted their conversation.

Everyone's left me! Patty thought. She ran out of the night club. She could feel her panic rising. She was struggling to wake up, but she was still asleep and she could see herself racing and racing, trying to find her family. She was afraid they'd left her behind. When she woke up, her heart hammered inside her. *I'm going to die,* she feared. She couldn't go back to sleep after that.

For weeks she continued to have trouble sleeping, and she was losing weight. "I don't mind losing weight," she confided in Richard, "but I've lost my appetite. And that's not good with all the training Dad and I are doing."

Because Patty's foot still bothered her, she was swimming eighty to one hundred laps in a pool several times a week to strengthen it. She was also running six to ten miles a day with her father, competing in girls' track, and riding her bike to train.

At home, when Patty tried to write letters or do her homework, she started to think about the run. When she tried to rest, thinking she'd take a nap, her fears would return. She couldn't concentrate on school and her grades were slipping.

Jim tried humoring her out of her fears. They could joke about them and Patty would feel fine, but then she'd break down unexpectedly and start weeping. She had been invited to attend several functions in conjunction with the run, but she begged her parents, "Please let me stay home!"

"We're going to have too many people with us on the trip," she confided to her mother. "I don't mind having John with us; he's part of the family. But Dad and I won't have any time alone. I enjoyed having runners with us during Portland, but Dad and I had the early morning to ourselves. No one came out at six. We had the last miles together. But now they've scheduled someone to run with us every single mile!"

"You're becoming too upset about this Patty," her mother answered. "I'm sure you'll have time alone with your father."

Patty scowled. "Maybe I'm just being selfish. I don't like sharing Daddy with anyone. I remember when he helped with girls' cross-country practice. He ran with the slowest girl to help her. It made me mad! I don't like people taking my dad away from me!"

"Oh, Patty. In a few days you and he will be flying to Minnesota for the press conferences. You know how you are; once you start running, you'll be fine!"

Patty remained silent; she couldn't admit to her mother everything that was bothering her. It would only worry her too much. Her left foot had really been hurting her, but she kept reminding herself that if she waited long enough the pain would go away. She was scared because she didn't know what she was headed for and what might happen to her on the run. Mostly she didn't want to miss two months of school. This was her senior year. She'd been elected Secretary of Athletics, but she wouldn't even be there to participate or to enjoy her new position. Sometimes she made herself sick thinking about all these things.

16 *Super Run*

ON JULY 23, Patty and Jim flew to the Midwest and then east over their projected route. They planned a series of airport stops in major cities to hold press conferences for pre-run publicity purposes. Patty flew from Minneapolis to Milwaukee and Chicago one day, then to Indianapolis and Cleveland the next. The following two days she was in Buffalo and Boston, then in New York City, Baltimore, and Washington D.C.

Patty liked the fly-over because it gave her a feel for the different cities and states along the route. She was relieved to see where she would be going; a positive anticipation and excitement replaced the fears that had tortured her.

She noted in her journal that the planning of this trip was more precautionary than any of her previous runs. To assure Patty's health and well-being, the EFA required an initial examination followed by periodic checkups. On July 29 she flew back to New York, where Jim and she underwent the extensive evaluation at the Preventive and Sports Medicine Center in City Island. They were examined by Dr. Norbert Sander, Jr., a sports medicine specialist and director of the center. A noted marathon runner, Dr. Sander is a training consultant to amateurs, professional athletes, and Olympians in the United States and in Europe. The summary of Patty's examination stated:

> Her preliminary medical evaluation—including complete physical examination, pulmonary function test, resting electrocardiogram, chest

x-ray and complete blood screening—placed her in excellent condition despite her life-long diagnosis of epilepsy. . . . Her maximum electrocardiogram treadmill stress test of twenty-four minutes ten seconds and oxygen consumption of 49.5 milliliters per kilo per minute was the best level of fitness yet reached at City Island for women.

It continued with a detailed outline of what Patty's schedule should be, how much liquid she should drink, and what her calorie intake should be—four to five thousand calories per day. It closed with the recommendation that Patty be seen by doctors at the Sports Medicine Center at monthly intervals throughout her trip. The pain in Patty's left foot had eased; and the doctors made a special insert for her shoe to ensure proper support.

Patty thought the treadmill stress test was especially boring. She was in a small, sterile room. She tried to focus on what little scenery she could see through a tiny narrow window. She was surprised and elated when she was told that she'd broken the women's record for both professional and amateur athletes on the treadmill by three minutes.

Dotty, Richard, Sam, and John Loftus joined Jim and Patty in Minnesota on the thirtieth of July. Two recreational vehicles had to be picked up in Chicago and driven to Minneapolis. One vehicle would be used for the family and the other one for press conferences. Richard volunteered to drive one back.

Although the gas tank on the RV Richard was driving registered full, it was empty. Richard found himself out of gas during a terrible rainstorm, stranded without money or maps. Molly, the second driver, didn't see Richard stop. She drove on, and didn't find him until six hours later.

"And you were afraid this trip was going to be boring!" Patty teased Richard when he finally arrived at their hotel.

There was nothing boring at all about their two thousand mile Super Run. Send-off day, August 5, was plagued with problems. When Patty passed the Allstate film crew, she turned to wave, twisting her ankle and wrenching her knee. At first she thought it was a minor injury, typical of her awkwardness. But as the miles wore on, Patty's knee really began to hurt her and she also developed a blood blister.

After John examined Patty's knee, he decided they would ice it to bring the swelling down. If she felt like she could, she would run minimum mileage the following day. John kept in touch daily, and sometimes hourly, with the doctors at the Sports Medicine Center. On Patty's fourth day out they requested that she be flown to New York. The doctor's diagnosis was that she had strained her lateral collateral ligament and would have to rest her knee for a week or more.

Celebrity runs and fun runs had already been scheduled along their route for fund-raising purposes. While they were waiting for Patty's knee to heal, the Wilson family flew to Rockford, Illinois, to attend one of these scheduled events.

Patty's appearance in Rockford gave her a feeling of what it was like to be a superstar. She was ushered into a back storeroom to wait for the start of the event. An enormous crowd was waiting for her, and when she went out to meet the people, they screamed her name.

John had to guard Patty when they squeezed through the crush of people to reach a police car where television, radio, and news people interviewed her on tape and on film. Many of the local radio celebrities who'd advertised the event were there to run. John Loftus stayed as close to Patty as he could to protect her from the people shoving and pushing to get to her.

Then Patty was put on the back of a Corvette convertible which led the group of runners. At the Colonial Village Shopping Mall where the run concluded, the Mayor presented Patty with a key to the city, a bouquet of roses, and a charm for her bracelet. The crowd was given new lyrics to "Hello Dolly," substituting Patty's name for Dolly's, and she blushed as they sang to her.

After Patty spoke briefly to the audience, she walked onto the runway of the stage, and the people reached out to touch her and shake her hand. When it was over it seemed like she was autographing everything, even T-shirts. Sam, the official family photographer for the trip, was everywhere taking pictures.

Despite the success of this event and continued publicity for their Super Run, Jim was distressed by the lengthy delay. For every day they didn't run, their journey was extended. Jim was anxious to put in the miles, but he didn't have the final authority on when Patty could run again.

On August 21, doctors at the Sports Medicine Center finally released Patty. She ran six miles her first day and seven her second. She experienced minimal pain. By the third day her knee was much improved, but Patty noticed that Jim was upset.

"Dad was easily irritated," she wrote in her journal. "He in turn got Sam to cry. Richard shut up and I was mad. Dad is hard to control on this trip. This year Dad has no control and it makes him nervous not to have any leverage or say (he has a say in everything). It's as if the project that Jim Wilson started has now been taken out of Jim Wilson's hands."

On August 29, twenty-four days after their send-off, Patty and Jim finally crossed over the Minnesota state line into Wisconsin. Wearing her baseball cap backwards, Patty sang and laughed and sometimes chanted, "No gain without pain."

"I'm so happy to get out of Minnesota!" Patty exclaimed to reporters. "I met some lovely people there, but we have to move on. We have to make progress. Besides—the mosquitos are terrible!"

When she was given the key to the city by the Mayor of La Crosse, Wisconsin, she thanked him, then grinned mischievously and quipped, "Does this key, by any chance, open the doors to those gas station restrooms that always seem to be locked?"

In cities and states along their route, there were numerous similar presentations, and Patty received eleven keys to the cities, charms for her bracelet, coins, scores of T-shirts, and bouquets of flowers. Twenty-four "Patty Wilson Days" were proclaimed. She was welcomed by countless political dignitaries—mayors, congressmen, senators, and governors—some of whom were no longer in office by the time she reached the finale in November.

She received footballs from the Washington Redskins, the Cleveland Browns, and the New England Patriots. The Milwaukee Bucks and the Indiana Pacers gave her basketballs. One of Patty's favorites,

Woody Hays—who was then football coach at Ohio State—gave her an autographed hat. The Cleveland Indians and the National Football League Players Association also gave her hats.

Innumerable newspaper journalists and television and radio personalities interviewed Patty, and she appeared on the *Good Morning Minnesota* and *Live at Five* shows. Some television stations ran informative documentaries about epilepsy along with their interviews with Patty. Others slotted her in with the daily news.

No matter how they chose to cover the story, the interviewers always amused Patty and Jim with their consistent astonishment: "She looks like a normal teenage girl!"

Jim's standard tongue-in-cheek response became, "Well, what did you expect? A third eye? Horns? Wings? Or should she be green?"

Patty also informed reporters, "The questions you ask about my life are an example of how uneducated the American public is about epilepsy. You really don't understand how my schooling has been. You just assume that I went to private school and that I've always been ridiculed because I have epilepsy, but these assumptions aren't true at all. I want everyone to know that people with epilepsy are normal and we do lead normal lives!"

Saturday, September 5, their one month anniversary, found the Wilsons in Tomah, Wisconsin. They had finally passed the 220-mile mark, and *Baraboo News Republic* sports editor Jim Schnetz summarized Patty's and Jim's feelings at this time.

Jim told him how much the people meant to him along the route. "Smaller cities generate the most warmth and generosity," he added. Patty spoke of the rivalry among the towns of Tomah, Sparta, and Mauston. In Sparta, the football team had run with Jim and Patty for nine miles. Then the high school gridders from Tomah accompanied them, completing an eleven mile jaunt to outdistance Sparta's team. Finally, a member of the Mauston High School team ran twelve miles to edge out Tomah's lead.

Patty talked about the goals Jim had set for her. "Dad holds too high an opinion of me," she said. "He has plans to develop a 'Patty Wilson Doll' who will walk, talk, and look like me." She told Schnetz that sometimes her father thinks of her as that doll. "I'm not a machine. . . . I'm Patty, and I'm human. When you bend my finger back it hurts. There are times when Dad doesn't think I can hurt."

Jim explained his viewpoint. "Some parents who have children with disorders tend to spoil them. They think they have to make it up in some way," he said. "Not so in the Wilson family."

The fun runs and celebrations were exciting, but once again it was the people of all ages—and especially the people with epilepsy—who came out to run with them, cheer them on, and support them who meant the most to Patty and Jim. Brenda, the mother of a nine-year-old boy, had a difficult time coping with the fact that she had epilepsy. When she heard Patty was coming, she was so excited she began to practice running. She had gone from door to door to neighbors to seek donations. She wasn't able to run more than a quarter of a mile, but the day she ran with Patty, the two were so absorbed in conversation that Brenda had covered over a mile before she realized it.

Everett Hartley and his grown daughter Louise ran with them. Louise had been injured in a tractor accident, and as a result of head injuries, she had brain damage and epilepsy. Richard and Sam stayed with Everett while Patty and Jim ran with Louise, who didn't understand about the running and wandered out in the middle of the road. In appreciation, Everett Hartley brought them fresh corn on the cob, gave a sizable donation, and his wife, Marie, treated the Wilson family to a sumptuous Wisconsin farm dinner.

In September, a woman whose brother had epilepsy before he died walked two miles with her dog to give Patty four silver dollars. Joan Kircher, from Massachusetts, hand-lettered a banner, that read, THANKS A MILLION FROM ONE OF 2 MILLION. Four hundred elementary school children worked for two days to locate Patty. They pinpointed her arrival, then waited and watched for her on Highway 40. When the children spotted the flashing red light of the Wilsons' sheriff's escort, they broke into cheers of "Run, Patty, run! Run, Patty, run!" Patty and Jim stopped briefly to shake their hands and thank them for cheering them on.

Some people who came out followed the Wilson family a full day's trek. In Delaware, Brian Anderson's father stayed with them for three days. Brian, a slender eight-year-old, had experienced seventeen drop seizures a day before the drug sodium vaolporate had been approved for use in the United States. Brian's chin was crisscrossed with hairline scars, and hematoma knots covered his forehead because he had blacked out and fallen on his face so often. Brian was so excited about Patty's coming that his father took him out of school to run with her. Brian had raised $109 for the Super Run all by himself.

With Brian, Patty came alive, smiling and encouraging him. She ran in a leaned-over position so she could talk with him. She watched him carefully and when she noticed him tiring, she'd signal for Brian's father to pick him up and let him ride in the car awhile. Brian wanted to be at Patty's finale in Washington, D.C., a trip he eventually made with his parents.

At the Pennsylvania-Delaware line, seventy-five people from an institution for the severely handicapped came out in their wheelchairs. To them Patty represented not only epilepsy, but was a champion of their rights and needs as well. They each wore *run Patty run* T-shirts, and when she shook their hands their faces lit up.

Jim asked one blind young man, "Do you want to meet Patty?"

A wide grin spread across his face. "Sure, I want to meet Patty!" He touched Patty, patted her, and hugged her as if he'd received a special gift. Tears filled Patty's and Jim's eyes, and bystanders were equally moved by the experience.

In Maryland, one runner had made a special chair with wheels for his young daughter who had cerebral palsy and epilepsy. He ran several miles with Patty and Jim, pushing his daughter along in the chair. There was camaradrie among the runners, and several of them took over for the father and pushed his daughter.

From Minnesota to Washington, D.C., members of the National Association for Girls and Women in Sports escorted Patty. In Maryland, Debbie Sears and Lori Sanford planned to run ten miles, but Jim challenged them to go the limit, a full thirty miles. Jim spent that day keeping Lori and Debbie psyched-up. When they made it, he shook their hands vigorously and congratulated them as if they'd run a thousand miles. Patty and Jim gave themselves day in and day out to the people, listening intently to them, chatting with them, urging them on, and keeping them going.

Patty's feelings about the Super Run were mixed. At times she enjoyed it; it was exciting and she felt good about it. Other times she thought about how much she missed being with her friends, dating, and participating in all of the extracurricular activities at school. She wondered if her Super Run were worth it, and if she were really helping people. If not, then what was she doing so far away from home? She composed a poem to express her grief and confusion.

> I sweat all day.
> I fret at night.
>
> I'm trying to bring
> a problem to light.
>
> But now I don't
> understand, exactly
> where I stand, I'm
> confused and don't know
> where I stand.

In mid-September she ran with Mayor Michael Bilandic of Chicago. At a picnic afterwards, people grabbed Patty and steered her from place to place to pose her with their children for pictures. She felt as if she were being manipulated like a doll, and she was overwhelmed by the whirling and turning and pushing and pulling. Then someone took Richard aside and told him that Patty was being "used by anyone and everyone who was smart enough to plug into the "Run Patty Wilson Super Run." It upset Patty because she felt she was to be used for the benefit of the epilepsy movement and not for personal gain.

When she wrote in her journal about feeling used, she asked herself, "Do you know how important that makes you feel? It makes you feel less important than an inanimate object. I cried all the way home . . . John was supposed to talk to me, but when we got back to the hotel John had to change a tire in the rain . . . That wasn't the only time I felt used," she added. "There were many other times."

But feeling used was not all that was distressing Patty. The total amount of $125,000 that was finally raised was far short of the projected two million dollars. Because Patty had especially wanted to raise money for research purposes, this was one of her major disappointments.

In October, Patty and Jim crossed the one thousand-mile mark in Strongville, Ohio. Then, nine days into the month, Patty had a convulsion while resting after lunch. The Wilsons phoned her neurologist in California, who advised them to have her blood level tested. Jim and Dotty took Patty to a physician who had attended her previous day's ceremonies in Cleveland. He examined her and said she would be fine, so Patty and Jim resumed running alone that evening to finish their last ten miles.

At seven-tenths of a mile, Patty had a second seizure. She fell to the ground, stopped breathing and started to turn blue. Jim was frightened, but she came to without any difficulty and her only complication was a severe headache.

The following morning the doctor advised them that the blood level of Patty's anti-convulsant medication was too low. Her dosage would have to be increased. He further recommended that she only run fifteen miles instead of her normal thirty, and that she should continue a reduced mileage for several days thereafter. Fortunately, Patty didn't have another seizure and she was able to go on as if she had never had one.

With the November elections a few days off, Rosalyn Carter was in Rochester, New York, to campaign for Governor Hugh Carey and meet Patty. The event was held in Midtown Plaza before more than a thousand people. After Mrs. Carter spoke about Governor Carey, she talked to Patty about epilepsy and her Super Run. Mrs. Carter closed by extending Patty an invitation to the White House, which thrilled Patty so much she spontaneously hugged Mrs. Carter. Then Patty thanked the First Lady and presented her with T-shirts for Amy, President Carter, and herself.

Patty was given a proclamation, a key to the city from Mayor Thomas P. Ryan, and checks from various organizations that had previously raised funds for her Super Run. Governor Carey presented Patty with a medal and an "I Love N.Y." T-shirt.

While Patty was making history—breaking her long-distance running record and being honored by Rosalyn Carter and other dignitaries—history was making itself. From the beginning of Patty's odyssey she shared bold black headlines and front page pictures of her Super Run with dramatic photos of the world's griefs and triumphs.

Over the three and a half months of her run, President Carter had been meeting with Prime Minister Menachem Begin of Israel and President Anwar Sadat of Egypt to negotiate agreements to provide for a full Middle East peace treaty. Across America there were the usual bleak reports of murder, crime, and inflation, as well as major fires, an earthquake, and a landslide, which destroyed homes and disrupted lives. Internationally, guerilla warfare flared into open rebellion in Nicaragua.

From August to October three popes headed the Catholic church. In November two great contributors to American culture, anthropologist Margaret Mead and artist Norman Rockwell, died. A week following the conclusion of Patty's run, the world was devastated with the news of the Jonestown suicide of over nine hundred people.

During their journey, the Wilsons also followed sports victories and defeats. Muhammad Ali beat Leon Spinks to win his heavyweight crown for the third time. The Wilsons were in New York at the height of World Series fever and watched the New York Yankees triumph over their California team, the Los Angeles Dodgers. Football season opened and Patty and her family were guests of the New England Patriots, who massacred the New York Jets fifty-six to twenty-one.

Other women, like Patty also attempted incredible feats of endurance. Diana Nyad undertook a swim from Cuba to Key West, Florida, while Stella Taylor tried a similar feat from the Bahamas to the Sunshine State. Thrashing waves and powerful currents defeated these women in their one hundred mile battle against the Atlantic Ocean.

Beverly Johnson became the first lone woman to scale the three-thousand-foot sheer granite wall of El Capitan in Yosemite, while Patty pushed faithfully toward her goal to become the youngest woman ever to run two thousand miles. Patty broke her Portland record of 1,310 miles between Newark and Lyons on October twentieth, finishing her day at 1,336.6 miles.

17 The Finale!

ROUTING the Super Run had been an intricate, complex undertaking. Some highways were long simple stretches, but in cities their routes were often as tricky and complicated as a maze. Jeff Darman, then president of the Road Runners Club of America, had been hired as a full-time consultant to coordinate their trip. The National Joggers Association also provided technical assistance.

Volunteers in each state drove sections of the route. They clocked the mileage on the odometer of their cars, marked maps, and recorded detailed descriptions of the road conditions, scenery, and landmarks.

These maps and instructions were thick and lengthy. Not only did the chosen route have to be direct, it had to bring Jim and Patty past city halls and state capitols. John Loftus often carried block-by-city-block instructions pinned to his shorts. He stayed in daily contact with Jeff Darman, who kept John updated on routing changes made because of construction, or in case a simpler, more direct route had been found.

On November 4, Patty stayed in her hotel for a day of rest while the rest of her family took a chauffeured limousine tour of New York City. Throughout the trip when her family went on sightseeing excursions or out to eat, Patty often remained behind, eating her meals in her room because she was fatigued. John usually stayed with her, and Patty relied more and more on him. He became her big brother, body guard, and counselor; with him, she discussed everything that upset her. John also saw to it that Patty was protected from the three-ring circus atmosphere of the Super Run. Jim, with his endless supply of energy and exuberance, thrived on the excitement and interviews, but the constant pressure drained and depressed Patty.

John acted as their public relations person, advising the people of Patty's schedule when they came out to see her, run with her, or interview her. To guard her physical health and mental well-being, John had to cut off interviews or cancel events if he felt it was going to be too much for her. He tried not to alienate anyone, but at the same time he had to fight constantly for Patty's privacy and rest. Toward the end of the run, John ran more and more with Patty. He was with her when she started out and when she was through. He carried her piggy-back to her starting or stopping spot, their special ritual.

Although Dotty, Richard, Sam, and John were a harmonious, hard working back-up team, John had the most exhausting, rigorous job of anyone connected with the run. In the morning he was up before the Wilsons and the last one in bed at night. He handled the monies, kept a record of expenses, checked the Wilsons in and out of hotels, kept track of the route, changed tires, and ran a total of 647.9 miles.

John was also liaison person between the Wilsons, EFA, and All-state. He buffered the tensions between them and listened to complaints from every direction, while still trying to solve problems and please everyone. John did the detailed planning, yet he always had to remain flexible enough to change those plans. He felt as if he were doing a daily balancing act on a tightrope.

John also had to contend with the constantly changing elements of the journey—the ebb and flow of traffic, the weather, terrain, road conditions, location, people, and Patty's and Jim's physical, mental, and emotional condition.

From Minnesota through Wisconsin, Illinois, Indiana, Ohio, Pennsylvania, New York, Massachusetts, Connecticut, and on to New Jersey, Delaware, Maryland, and Washington, D.C., Patty and Jim ran through a cross-section of America. They might be in a hamlet, or farm country, or wilderness, or small town in the morning, and in a heavily congested metropolis in the afternoon. They ran past immaculate, pastured farms and past neglected farms with decaying barns. They passed through slums, dangerous high crime areas, and wealthy, exclusive districts.

Patty and Jim passed hospitals, factories, schools, and colleges. They saw small white steepled churches, enormous stone cathedrals, and historical sights and monuments. They hurried by cemeteries with standing stone monuments and antique stores selling ancient treasures.

They experienced every kind of weather in their zig-zag across the Midwest and Northeast, from blistering heat and steaming humidity to drenching rains and cold crisp winds. Summer evenings gradually changed from casually-lighted days to formal shades of autumn gray. At roadside stands, refreshing watermelons were sold in August, to be replaced with crisp red apples and golden pumpkins in October. Green summer corn with shiny silken heads turned to stiff beige stalks by fall. Lavish green-leafed maples, birches and elms burst into flaming shades of yellow, orange, scarlet, and golden brown.

Patty and Jim crossed wide-bridged rivers and placid streams that cut through the land. They passed quiet meadows and deep dark woods, pasture lands and furrowed fields, sparsely forested slopes and tree-lined creeks. In the summer, children laughed and shrieked, playing in the lakes and rivers. In the fall these bodies of water were brown and cold and leaf-laden.

Patty appreciated the quietness of the countryside. Often only a covey of birds fluttering out of the brush, or the occasional whisper of tires clacking across a rut in the road could be heard. It was a tranquil contrast to the cities. There the bang and clash of traffic, the beeping, honking, and gear-grinding, the screaming wail of fire engines and ambulances, the rhythmic clack of trains rumbling onward were the instruments of a discordant orchestra. Every variety of bus, truck, and car started and stopped, screeched and roared, skidded and whipped by Patty and Jim. They choked on the sickening stench of exhaust fumes.

When Patty and Jim passed by, people waiting for buses or walking down the sidewalks gawked and strained to read the inscription on their T-shirts advertising their Super Run. Sometimes Patty and Jim ran alone with their family. Ultimately Richard ran 669.9 miles,

Sam ran 441.8, and Dotty 295.1 miles to keep Patty and Jim company and boost their morale.

Other times Patty and Jim were pied pipers, leading runners ahead of bumper-to-bumper traffic held back by a police escort. Some officers escorted them silently; one talked to Patty and Jim over the loud speaker and sang to them to keep them going. Another, Bill, knew the history of his valley and surrounding area and pointed out sights like a tour guide.

Patty and Jim journeyed through the inner cities, where skyscrapers deflected the sunlight, making the narrow streets seem like a dark cavern. In older sections, proprietors maintained their businesses as if it were 1948 instead of 1978. Some schools were barred and fenced, with playgrounds on the roof. People with briefcases hawked their wares or solicited others to join their particular brand of religion.

In the slums the runners passed hot dog stands with faded signs where pigeons scratched for leftovers. There were sleazy bars, greasy hamburger joints, and blinking neon signs. Graffiti spattered the walls. Rusting cars stood abandoned. Cans vomited foul-smelling garbage. The windows on paint-peeled buildings were cracked or boarded, and water-stained curtains hung in shreds from tenement windows.

A tattered wino slumped against a stoop. A young woman danced and weaved down the middle of the street, waving her cigarette and chattering incoherently to some unknown demon. A drug deal was quickly transacted. A blind man, tapping his red and white cane, held out a cup and begged.

While Patty and Jim ran, they observed and photographed these sights in their minds, but like the lens of a camera, they captured only partial pictures of the panoramic whole, while other sights were forgotten.

The sights, sounds, and smells of their surroundings saturated their thoughts until they wondered if they could absorb anymore. But when Patty and Jim were running, their minds could slip beyond the noise-infested world to a state of altered consciousness. The thump, thump, thump of their footfalls was a peaceful steady motion, a hypnotic rhythm. Their lightly clenched fingers, their forearms pumping forward and back, synchronized with their stride. Often it gave them a feeling of floating, of gliding across pavement. This was the runner's high—a feeling of elation, a mystical ecstasy. Intense, sensuous, spiritual, euphoric, it was an acute sensitivity.

There were also phychic benefits. They meditated, identified, created, philosophized, and perceived life beyond the threshold of their consciousness. They sifted ideas, and panned for that golden fleck of insight. Although at times running darkened their feelings and they felt as if it would drain their sanity, more often it cleansed their minds and renewed their spirits.

Running heightened fantasy, while at the same time it expanded reality. For Jim it was Superman's flight, swishing through the air, moving faster than the speed of sound, becoming the man of steel. There was always that inner tension, that unconscious alert system programmed for emergency.

Running was the definition of their life. It was an addiction, and Patty and Jim would never be able to quit without pain or an undefined feeling of loss.

During the last whirlwind week, Patty and her family had been graciously received by Rosalyn Carter at the White House. Immediately following, Patty was honored at the Touchdown Club where Roy Jefferson, former Washington Redskins football star, emceed the luncheon. Allstate Life Insurance President Jack O'Laughlin and Executive Vice-President Al McNichol represented their company, which was honored for underwriting the expenses of the Super Run. Patty received a bronzed shoe from Nike shoe company. Brig Owens gave her a topaz NFL Players Association ring—a special honor, since she is the only person outside the ranks of professional football players to own one.

Two days to Washington, D.C.—only 41.2 miles to the finish. Patty and Richard were running together. Ordinarily they talked when they ran, but now they were unusually quiet as they passed the Maryland woods. The day before, a feeling of foreboding had distressed Richard. It had started with a mere suggestion. No vague fear, this was real—a chilling thought, a terror they had encountered before. He hadn't said anything to Patty about it because he hadn't had time to talk to her privately.

He glanced at her as they ran, trying to decide how to voice his feelings. When he spoke the words escaped, at first haltingly, then boldly announcing the premonition.

"Jeff and I were talking, and he was saying to me, 'We've made it almost two thousand miles. Wouldn't it be a shame if something happened to Patty—if she were hit by a car?'"

Patty looked up at her brother, her expression dispassionate, curious.

"After making it this far," Richard continued, "after all the hardships we've been through, what if we never finished, this close to the end?"

Patty laughed and said lightly, "We've almost been nailed so many times it isn't funny!" Unconsciously, she stroked her face, wiping away the perspiration. Her silver barrettes failed to restrain wispy strands of hair; her single braid wagged down her back like the tail of a friendly puppy.

They were facing traffic, with Richard at the outside. His blue baseball cap unsuccessfully tried to tame his mass of curly hair. Patty was running next to the low stone wall of a bridge. She was thinking about school and a project she'd like to initiate as Secretary of Athletics.

Farther down, Richard noticed a car cross the white line, then the shoulder. He expected it to stop, but it didn't. He hesitated. This break in rhythm woke Patty from the magic of her imagination. She glanced up to see the car rushing toward them, straddling the sidewalk along the bridge.

Patty and Richard froze! They were unable to wave or shout at the driver in hopes he would see them. There was no time or space to jump. They pressed themselves against the stone wall. The car lunged at them!

He's going to nail us! Richard's thoughts screamed.

They could see the man's face as the car swerved, brushing them as it passed. Had the middle-aged driver seen them or not? They couldn't tell. He appeared dazed, perhaps drunk. Patty and Richard turned instinctively and watched. The man was jerking and bouncing inside the car, which careened off the bridge and lurched onto the grass. The car finally halted, perched at the edge of the woods. Another car pulled in behind and the occupants scrambled out to check on the injured driver.

Patty and Richard had broken their stride just for those brief moments. Numbly, they kept moving. When they spotted a police car on the opposite side of the road, the initial shock started to wear off.

"We should tell the policeman about the accident," Richard finally spoke.

"We should! I wonder if the man was hurt? He almost killed us." Patty's voice was curiously flat. She looked up at Richard. He was pale. *Poor guy, I don't think he's going to live,* she thought. *I'll try to make him laugh.*

"You must be scared! Your hair went straight!" she giggled.

"We'd better watch the traffic," suggested Richard soberly.

"In case any more crazy drivers try to knock us off." chuckled Patty. "Hey, there's the RV!"

Their motor home was parked a couple blocks ahead of them, on the other side of the highway. Instinctively, they quickened their pace; home was in sight.

Then, without warning, a county truck started to make a U-turn in the middle of the road. The driver swung out so far that the truck was sweeping right at them.

"Patty!" Richard yelled.

The orange truck nearly clipped them both, but Patty scurried on as if this second near miss were an every day experience. Richard, still dazed, watched her. She appeared so calm, so cool. He knew she was scared, maybe as scared as he was. She'd escaped vehicles coming at her thousands of times before, but how could she let it go by so casually? The way the car and truck came at them, death seemed certain. He wondered if these close, brief encounters with death numbed her to its reality. An overwhelming awe, rather than relief, spread through Richard. Spontaneously, his flesh twitched; a spasm coursed through his body.

A tepid breeze caressed Patty's face and brushed her hair. An unexpected grief surged up inside her. The premonition seemed more real, more true, than she cared to accept. What if she were hit, or her father, or her brother, or one of the other runners? What if they didn't complete the 2,000 mile run? Two days from the finish! Wasn't this super run supposed to prove that people with epilepsy can live normal lives? She couldn't help wondering if she had accomplished that.

Even so, she wanted more than anything else to celebrate her seventeenth birthday flying hand in hand with her father to the finish! Whatever strife there had been, whatever peril she had faced, however much pain and fatigue she had borne, she did not want that final moment of triumph scarred or the joy of it broken.

Patty spotted her father resting at the side of the road, watching, waiting for Richard and her to catch up to him. She drew in a long, deep breath; it was a relief to see her father. Suddenly, she felt unusually elated and safe. *We're going to make it!* she assured herself.

November 16, the Wilson team was tense and keyed up, especially Patty. She couldn't contain her nervousness, or the flow of energy that always came before a long-fought-for goal. It had been her longest journey, 104 days since her send-off on a warm summer's day in Minnesota. Now it was a chilling fifty degrees, a raw gray morning in Washington, D.C.

For warmth, Patty wore two T-shirts; the white one stuck out underneath her scarlet red one like collar and cuffs, and her silky purple shorts were a colorful match. Her only concession to the rain-threatening sky was a red knit cap, rimmed in white. Her sun-bronzed skin was a striking contrast to the winter-white bystanders bundled in raincoats. Jim and Rich wore bright gold shirts and John was in brilliant orange—they would run these last miles with her.

The curbs and sidewalks were banked to overflowing with rain soaked leaves. The trees lining the street were brown scraggly whisk brooms propped on the ends of their handles. A squad of police vehicles escorted Patty's entourage, their globes blinking and circling.

Patty had attracted a collection of track teams and running clubs, which filled their ranks at different points along the fourteen-and-a-half mile route. Children with developmental disabilities joined them. One of the most spirited, inspiring contingents was a twenty-man honor guard from the US Marine Corps. They chanted a steady cadance of songs and cheers, rousing the runners' spirits.

At the 3.6 mile mark, a large group of runners fell in step with them, swelling their numbers to well over a hundred. Their cheeks and noses were apple-colored and their breath rose in frosty puffs. They were too excited to complain about the bone-chilling cold or their water-soaked shoes and feet. Perspiration curled strands of hair at their necks.

Dignitaries who would honor Patty officially in a few moments were honoring her with the highest of all compliments; they were running with her. James Autry, then president of EFA, ran with Patty in Minnesota and Chicago. He would present her with an EFA achievement trophy cup. New Mexico's governor Jerry Apodaca, chairman of the President's Council on Physical Fitness, would honor her with a citation from his office. Jeff Darman would drape a beribboned gold medal around her neck because "she deserves one, even if it isn't the Olympics." Her physician, Dr. Norbert Sander, Jr., Roy Jefferson and his daughter, and Brig Owens had already honored her in previous ceremonies and they were beside her.

On Embassy Row, officials from foreign embassies lined both sides of Massachusetts Avenue. The dignified buildings were a stately frame for this brilliantly colored moving picture of runners. When Patty passed different embassies, staff members dashed into the street to hand Patty miniature flags from their countries. At the Libyan Embassy children dressed in Super Run T-shirts cheered: "Run, Patty, run! Run, Patty, run!" Generous waves and rousing applause followed her.

Spirits were even higher now, giddy and jubilant, yet there was an underlying seriousness and respect for Patty. Some had worked with her for this great victory. Her charm and her genuine sense of purpose had drawn a circle of warmth around this enormous group of runners. They were honored to be with her, and almost overcome by their elation.

People of every age strained against the ropes, watching for Patty. The White House—fenced off like a royal palace—stood directly opposite Lafayette Park where the crowd awaited Patty's appearance.

Dotty and her parents, Sam, Jim's mother Helen, and Nana were already on the grandstands waiting with the crowd. Blue, white, and green-furled flags—fluttering in the breeze—were held at attention on each side of the L-shaped aisle. The crowd spotted the swarm of runners in the distance and a cheer went up for them. An area in the front was sectioned off for the TV cameramen and journalists; they hissed and elbowed and jockeyed for the best position to capture her moment of triumph.

Patty and Jim stepped up on the curb and gripped hands. They bent their heads slightly forward. Their legs reached up and out and they swooped down the aisle. Two children held a paper banner with sharp blue letters announcing, "FINISH LINE." Patty and Jim broke through the banner, leaving each half fluttering behind them, and were whisked up on to the grandstand.

An enormous smile tugged at the corners of Patty's mouth, and she waved her fistful of flags. It was a moment electric with emotion for the hundreds who had run with her and for those who had waited so eagerly. The applause and cheering rang louder and louder.

Patty was breathless and numb, not so much from the damp cold, but from the excitement. She started to shiver all over. Her mother handed her soft blue sweats and she gratefully put them on.

Wave after wave of applause went up for her. Behind her a flock of birds fluttered, then swept upward together as if someone had released them for this moment in her celebration. Jim's eyes filled and he found himself crying. Nana wept beside him. He watched his daughter with a great sense of pride and an infinite tenderness. Sam and Richard and John and Dotty and the others on the stand were clapping enthusiastically for her.

Patty's eyes swept over the crowd; there wasn't a hint of shyness in her. Her face was radiant, full of life, and her friendliness was a beautiful thing.

"It sure took us a long time to get here," Patty finally spoke. "A hundred days on the road! A lot of people have come into our lives because of this. I don't really know what to say except to thank everyone." Patty drew in her breath. "We made it!" she grinned broadly and held up her flags. "Just like we said in the beginning!"

Epilogue

WHEN Patty returned to high school, it seemed like the emptiest of her four years; she didn't feel a part of it anymore. It may have been because her brother, Richard, her closest friends, and a boy she had been dating steadily had already graduated. It may have been, she later explained, because "it was hard for me to come off the Super Run where I had to grow up fast and then step back down into the role of a senior in high school."

Patty attended several "after the run" fund-raising dinners. Their various hosts included the Los Angeles Rams, the Cleveland Browns, and the Cleveland Indians. George Allen and champions from the 1972 Washington Redskins also served as masters of ceremony. Jim and Patty then flew to Florida to attend a Celebrity Golf Tournament, hosted by NBC's Frank Blair. They also went to New Orleans, where they received plaques from the National Association for Sports and Physical Education.

In June, when Patty graduated, she had oddly mixed feelings of relief and bewilderment. "Finally it's over," she said, "but what do I do next?"

More than anything, she hoped to find her place in the crowd and to continue her active dating and social life, which she preferred to being in the spotlight. Beyond that, Patty knew she wanted to attend college. She had received a scholarship from the Epilepsy Foundation of America in recognition of all she had done to increase public awareness and understanding of epilepsy.

As for running, she doesn't know what to expect. She would still like to run from New York to Los Angeles, like her father and she planned in the beginning. Various other runs have been proposed by and to the Wilsons, including running the lengths of England, New Zealand, and Switzerland.

Before their Washington, D.C., run, which Patty felt was simply "Portland grown up," she thought she had a close but average family. But "it was during the Super Run," she says, "that our family became a unit."

PATTY WILSON'S LONG-DISTANCE RUNS

La Palma to Los Angeles: January 1, 1975; thirty miles.

Los Angeles Marathon: March 22, 1975; completed twenty miles.

La Palma to San Diego: May 1, 1975, to May 4, 1975; Five days; one hundred miles.

Palos Verdes Marathon: June 14, 1975; completed twenty miles.

La Palma to Las Vegas: December 20, 1975, to December 30, 1975; eleven days; 300 miles.

La Palma to San Francisco: June 11, 1976, to June 29, 1976; nineteen days; 502.18 miles.

Pikes Peak Marathon: August 1, 1976; 14.2 miles; bronze medal for fourteen-to-nineteen-year-olds; silver medal for father and daughter.

Palos Verdes Marathon: June 11, 1977; twenty-six miles, 385 yards.

Buena Park, California to Portland, Oregon: June 18, 1977, to July 29, 1977; forty-two days; 1,310.5 miles.

Minneapolis, Minnesota, to Washington, D.C.: August 5, 1978, to November 16, 1978 (Patty's seventeenth birthday); 104 days, ninety-two days running; 2,009.4 miles.

It was the first preseason cross-country event in La Mirada, California. Patty Wilson was the only girl among fifty runners, and at thirteen, she was one of the youngest.

When the gunshot cracked the air, Patty dashed out with the front group of runners. The last thing she recalled was her father reminding her not to start off too fast; after that she didn't remember anything. A quarter mile out, Patty started running mechanically, her arms and legs swinging stiffly. She didn't seem to be breathing; her chest was still, giving no sign that she was inhaling or exhaling.

Despite her marching, mechanical style, she sped past boys who were stretching up and out for the final burst across the line.

Patty darted across the finish line in ninth place. Her coach, her teammates, and her family congratulated her. They didn't know Patty had had a partial complex seizure. She appeared to respond to their congratulations. She seemed to be conscious, but she wasn't: she was completely unaware of what was happening. Like a dazed boxer, she was knocked out, but still standing.

Patty Wilson has always been a fighter. At age sixteen, she ran 1,310 miles from Buena Park in southern California, to Portland, Oregon, refusing to let mental or physical obstacles stop her. After forty-two days she reached Portland, setting the world distance record for women runners.

Patty Wilson has epilepsy; she suffers from a little-understood disorder of the nervous system that causes seizures and partial or total loss of consciousness. For too many people, that means she shouldn't attempt simple sports, let alone running. But Patty vows, "I haven't been stopped because of epilepsy. I never will."